# AMERICAN LEGENDS OF THE WILD WEST

# AMERICAN LEGENDS OF THE WILD WEST

RICHARD MANCINI

COURAGE BOOKS
AN IMPRINT OF
RUNNING PRESS
PHILADELPHIA, PENNSYLVANIA

Canadian Representatives:
General Publishing Co., Ltd.
30 Lesmill Road, Don Mills
Ontario M3B 2T6

9 8 7 6 5 4 3 2 1
Digit on the right indicates the number
of this printing.

Library of Congress
Cataloging-in-Publication Number
91-58653

ISBN 1-56138-119-5

This book was designed and produced by
Quintet Publishing Limited
6 Blundell Street
London N7 9BH

Creative Director: Richard Dewing
Designer: Chris Dymond
Project Editor: Damian Thompson
Editor: Joy Wotton
Picture Research: Ibid Editorial Services

Typeset in Great Britain by
Central Southern Typesetters, Eastbourne
Manufactured in Hong Kong by
Regent Publishing Services Limited
Printed in Hong Kong by
Leefung-Asco Printers Limited

First Published by Courage Books
an imprint of Running Press Book Publishers
125 South Twenty-second Street
Philadelphia, Pennsylvania 19103

# CONTENTS

# INTRODUCTION

“The Wild West.” The phrase conjures up visions of vast expanses of breathtaking terrain populated by a host of determined pioneers, rugged cowboys, ruthless outlaws, fearless lawmen, proud Indian warriors and victorious cavalrymen – mythic images that grew along with the young United States of America as its borders moved westward throughout the 19th century.

What is perhaps most amazing about the mythic West, however, is that many of its legends still seem fresh in our memory, a full century after noted historian Frederick Jackson Turner declared the American frontier officially “closed”. And although those 100 years have seen an incredible array of changes in the landscape, life style and technology of the United States, the stories of the men and women who helped build it – and in some cases tried to tear it down – continue to fascinate and entertain us as we stand poised to enter the 21st century.

**BELOW** A fleeting symbol of the expanding American West, “tent cities” such as this one sprung up across the Western plains to support the building of the Transcontinental Railroad. This 1868 view depicts the “main street” of Benton, Wyoming, which provided goods to the crews of the westward-bound Union Pacific Railroad.

In the following pages you will meet scores of "legendary" personalities – ranging from the famous to the obscure – who either helped to shape, contributed a story to, or perhaps merely served as a footnote to the history of the American West. Although the period of the "Wild West" is often thought of as the years between the end of the Civil War and the beginning of the 20th century, the push westward actually began in the middle of the 18th century – even before the American Revolution. Consequently, this book will also include accounts of people and events from this earlier time when the American frontier was still considerably east of the Mississippi River and the nation was comprised of the original 13 colonies.

Because the saga of the American West can aptly be described as "sweeping", no single volume of this kind can begin to include all of the important and/or colorful personages who contributed to the West's considerable legends. I have therefore attempted to provide you with a sampling of personalities and events, arranged as chronologically as possible, within chapters that cover distinct categories – explorers, scouts, etc. And although "legends" are often grains of truth that have been "embellished" by folklore and gross exaggeration over time, I have tried to present historically accurate portrayals of the men and women of the "Wild West" – with a bit of popular legend added for fun, as well as for comparison.

**BELOW** Cattlemen contemptuously referred to settlers as "nesters", and tried to drive them off the range. This nester family was photographed on the range of the Three Block Ranch near Richardson, New Mexico, around 1905.

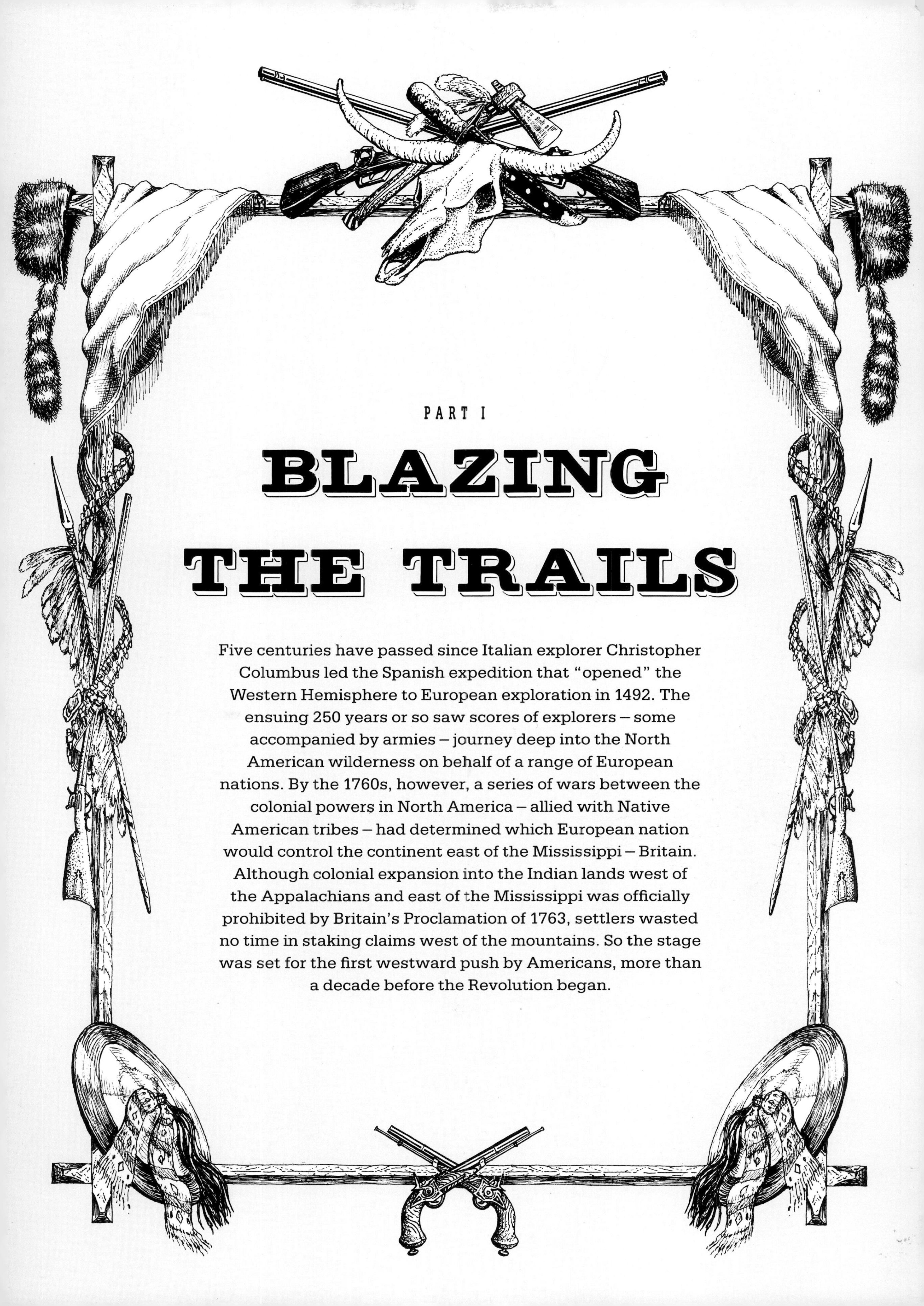

PART I

# BLAZING THE TRAILS

Five centuries have passed since Italian explorer Christopher Columbus led the Spanish expedition that "opened" the Western Hemisphere to European exploration in 1492. The ensuing 250 years or so saw scores of explorers – some accompanied by armies – journey deep into the North American wilderness on behalf of a range of European nations. By the 1760s, however, a series of wars between the colonial powers in North America – allied with Native American tribes – had determined which European nation would control the continent east of the Mississippi – Britain. Although colonial expansion into the Indian lands west of the Appalachians and east of the Mississippi was officially prohibited by Britain's Proclamation of 1763, settlers wasted no time in staking claims west of the mountains. So the stage was set for the first westward push by Americans, more than a decade before the Revolution began.

# EXPLORERS AND FRONTIERSMEN

## The Ultimate Frontiersman: Daniel Boone

Of the scores of men who led expeditions and founded settlements on the American frontier in the late 18th and early 19th centuries, perhaps none has enjoyed as legendary a reputation as Daniel Boone (1734–1820). Even today, Boone's name can evoke the image of the ultimate frontiersman – big, strong, savvy in the ways of the woods and utterly fearless – and brings to mind the many legends surrounding the man. Many of them are, in fact, pure bunk. But there is enough evidence to suggest that, all bunk aside, Daniel Boone was indeed a remarkable man.

Born a Pennsylvania Quaker, Boone grew to manhood on the North Carolina frontier. Although not large (only about 5′9″ tall), he was strong and agile, with a quick mind and an ability to think on his feet – attributes which served him well in the wilds of the south-east. Although Boone garnered early military experience against French and Indian troops in the ill-fated British assault on Fort Duquesne (now Pittsburgh) in 1755 – and would gain an inflated reputation as an "Indian fighter" two decades later – he learned his wilderness skills from friendly Native Americans whose ways he respected and understood.

It was in Kentucky, however, that Boone's legend grew and prospered. He first explored the region during the winter of 1767–8 and

**ABOVE** Today, tourists enjoy this view of the Appalachians from the Cumberland Gap – nearly $2\frac{1}{4}$ centuries after Daniel Boone and a company of axmen hacked the Wilderness Road through the pass in 1775, on their way to settling the new territory of Kentucky.

**OPPOSITE** A man truly ahead of his time, Daniel Boone was the prototype of the Western frontier trailblazer, taming the Appalachian wilderness during America's Revolutionary period. Although Boone's legendary exploits occurred in the years between the French and Indian War and the Louisiana Purchase, they set an example for the mountain men who were just striking out to the Rockies and beyond at the time of Boone's death in 1820.

continued between 1769 and 1771, at which time he crossed through the Cumberland Gap. In 1775, after mediating the purchase of 20 million acres of Kentucky Cherokee land, which was about to be opened to white settlers as the 14th colony, Transylvania, the 40-year-old Boone led 30 axemen to blaze a trail. Driving northward from Tennessee through the Cumberland Gap to the Kentucky River, they cleared the famous Wilderness Road, which ended at a settlement on the Kentucky they named Boonesboro.

When the American Revolution began, the "great frontiersman" took on a new role as a militia leader charged with directing the defense of Kentucky's frontier settlements against British and Indian attacks. Captured by Shawnees on a 1778 salt-gathering trek, Boone convinced his Indian captors to hold him and his men hostage – and stalled a Shawnee raid on defenseless women and children left in Boonesboro. After escaping, Boone reached Boonesboro in time to help fight off a British and Indian attack, but he later faced charges of treason for dealing with the Shawnee and the British. He was acquitted, and his legend grew to epic proportions after the Revolution.

Myths about Boone's prowess as an "Indian fighter" abounded and multiplied even in his own time. In fact, Boone never relished fighting Native Americans and may have killed only one Indian during his entire career. The real Boone was soft-spoken, intelligent and devoted to his family. His schooling was limited and his spelling atrocious, but he could read and write. And contrary to myth he never wore a "coonskin cap".

During his long life, Daniel Boone mastered many skills, but business was not among them. Over the years he earned or claimed many thousands of acres of land, but he lost most of them due to legal snags. When he died at the age of 85 in Missouri he did manage to leave land to his heirs. But his greatest legacy is, perhaps, his undying legend as the first trail-blazer of America's advance to the West coast.

# The Trek That Started It All: The Lewis and Clark Expedition

**BELOW** Meriwether Lewis was mysteriously and fatally shot in 1809 while serving as governor of the Louisiana Territory – just three years after completing the extraordinary expedition he planned and co-commanded with William Clark. Jefferson thought it to be suicide, while Clark and others came to believe Lewis was murdered.

In 1800, Louisiana – stretching from the western banks of the Mississippi River to the eastern slopes of the Rockies – was back in the control of its original claimants, the French. While Napoleon Bonaparte had little money to spend on its development, US President Thomas Jefferson recognized the vital importance of controlling the Mississippi – especially the port of New Orleans. When, in 1803, Jefferson moved to purchase New Orleans, Bonaparte countered by offering the entire territory – and Jefferson bought it.

The Louisiana Purchase, which doubled the land area of the United States, coincided with a Congressional appropriation for a pet project of Jefferson's that had been planned for some time – an expedition along the Missouri River and further west to discover a link between the Mississippi and the Pacific. The mission to find what many called the "North-west Passage" now had a second purpose: the exploration of the vast, unknown and uncharted Louisiana Territory.

To lead this historic trek to "the Western Sea", Jefferson chose an extremely able young friend and neighbor from his native Virginia, US Army captain Meriwether Lewis (1774–1809). Lewis, an intellectual with wilderness experience gained from a boyhood largely spent on the Georgia frontier, was also Jefferson's private secretary for a time. Although barely 30, he proved remarkably adept at planning, training and equipping an expedition that today might be comparable to a mission of interplanetary exploration. His own considerable knowledge of frontier and military ways was supplemented by pre-expedition "crash courses" in subjects including botany and Indian customs.

To serve as co-commander of his "Corps of Discovery", Lewis called upon another Virginia native and comrade-at-arms, William Clark (1770–1838), giving him equal authority on the expedition. An Army lieutenant who had gained his frontier savvy in the wilds of Kentucky, the vigorous Clark complemented the introspective Lewis perfectly, and shared his enthusiasm for and dedication to the dangerous mission ahead. The pair carefully chose 30 tough, experienced soldiers and frontiersmen possessing various skills as hunters, trappers, boatmen, carpenters and smiths; York, Clark's huge, powerful black slave, also accompanied the party and proved extremely valuable (he was freed by Clark after returning home). Equipped with a 60-foot keelboat, several smaller craft, "state-of-the-art" paraphernalia (some specially designed for the mission), gifts and trade items for the Native Americans it was sure to encounter, and enough provisions to support it for two years, the Corps of Discovery departed its base near St Louis on May 14, 1804.

Throughout the difficult journey, Clark assumed responsibility for navigation, mapping the terrain, maintaining discipline and handling diplomacy with the Indians. He often remained with the boats as they slowly progressed up the Missouri, while Lewis proceeded along the banks on foot, hunting, collecting specimens and making notes and sketches of the flora, fauna and natural features he observed. The party reached the mouth of the Platte River and held its first council with Indians – representatives of the Omaha, Missouri and Oto tribes – in July 1804 at what is today Council Bluffs, Iowa. They presented the chiefs with medals depicting Jefferson, the "Great Father" in Washington.

Through successfully standing up to a challenge by the formidable Teton Sioux chief Black Buffalo without firing a shot in September 1804, Lewis and Clark won the respect of many tribes they would later encounter. Setting up winter camp among the friendly Mandans in present-day North Dakota, they took on a French-Canadian fur trapper, Toussaint Charbonneau, and his 16-year-old Shoshoni wife, Sacajawea. Although her husband proved to be of little use to the expedition, this courageous young Native American woman has rightly been recognized as one of its most valuable members; as an interpreter and guide, she would save the party from disaster more than once.

Breaking camp in April 1805, the Corps of Discovery continued up the Missouri, reaching the Great Falls (in present-day Montana) in June, and the start of a 25-day portage to avoid nearly 20 miles of dangerous rapids. But the most grueling leg of the journey lay ahead, through one of the continent's most formidable natural barriers – the Rocky

**ABOVE** His exemplary service as co-commander of the "Corps of Discovery" was just the beginning of a long, splendid career for William Clark, shown here in Charles Willson Peale's companion painting to the portrait of Lewis. Clark's diplomatic skill among Native American leaders – who called him the "Red-Haired Chief" – led to his later appointment as the US Government's Superintendent of Indian Affairs.

**LEFT** The Shoshoni teenager Sacajawea, depicted here wading along the Pacific shore, proved to be of inestimable help to Meriwether Lewis and William Clark on their epic journey of Western exploration in 1804–06.

# IN THE SHADOW OF LEWIS AND CLARK: THE TRAVELS OF ZEBULON PIKE

**ABOVE** The mountain that Zebulon Pike claimed to be unscalable when he reached the Rockies in 1806 was conquered seven years after his death – in 1819. Pike's Peak, as it became known, was usually the first landmark seen by the new settlers as they made their way across the prairie, and the cry of Colorado gold prospectors was "Pike's Peak or bust!"

While Lewis and Clark were engaged in their legendary journey on behalf of President Jefferson, a much less honorable authority – General James Wilkinson, the devious, unscrupulous Governor of the Louisiana Territory who plotted treason with Aaron Burr, commissioned two other expeditions into Louisiana between 1805 and 1807. Both were led by Lieutenant Zebulon Montgomery Pike (1779–1813), a New Jersey-born officer in Wilkinson's command; in the first, his purpose was to explore the upper reaches of the Mississippi and in the second, the south-western portion of the territory bordering on Spain's North American possessions.

Pike's first expedition moved northward up the Mississippi by keelboat from St Louis on August 9, 1805. One of its objectives was to ensure that Canadian fur trappers – who were working for British companies – stayed out of US territory. After working his way upriver and holding council with Minnesota Sioux in September, Pike set up winter camp at Little Falls. On a trip in December 1805, to discover the source of the "Father of Rivers" (which he later incorrectly determined to be Minnesota's Leech Lake, instead of Lake Itasca), Pike and his men nearly froze to death. They survived only after finding shelter at Canadian trading posts – and then ungratefully demanded payment from the Canadians for doing business on American soil. The expedition returned to St Louis in the spring of April 1806 – and Pike soon received orders from Wilkinson to prepare for another journey in the summer, along the south-west border of the territory.

Pike's south-western trek proved far more valuable, but no less dangerous, than his Mississippi adventure. The expedition set out by barge from St Louis on July 15, 1806, moved westward up the Osage River, then overland across the Kansas and along the Arkansas. Reaching the southern Rockies in modern Colorado in November, Pike and some of his men tried to scale a 14,000-foot mountain,

but gave up, declaring it unclimbable. Caught somewhat unprepared for a bitter winter in the South-west, the party was forced to seek shelter in Spanish territory. Eventually captured by Spanish authorities, Pike and his men were taken to Santa Fe, then ushered backed into the US through what would later become Texas, returning to St Louis in 1807.

Zebulon Pike's reports of his south-western expedition, compiled mostly from memory (since his notes were captured by the Spaniards), prompted traders to seek out new business in Spanish territory and ultimately establish the Santa Fe Trail. His mistaken opinion that the south-western plains were a desert wasteland, however, kept settlers out of the region for years. Brigadier-General Pike was killed in Ontario during the War of 1812. Seven years after his death, the Colorado mountain that Pike declared unclimbable was conquered at last; later it became his final legacy to his country – Pike's Peak.

Mountains. As the expedition approached the mountains, Lewis and a patrol crossed the Continental Divide and ran into a band of Shoshoni. Sacajawea – who had been captured and taken from her Shoshoni family as a child – discovered that her brother was chief of the band. This stroke of luck secured the Shoshoni's help in obtaining the pack-horses necessary to cross the mountains, which the party did with great difficulty in September.

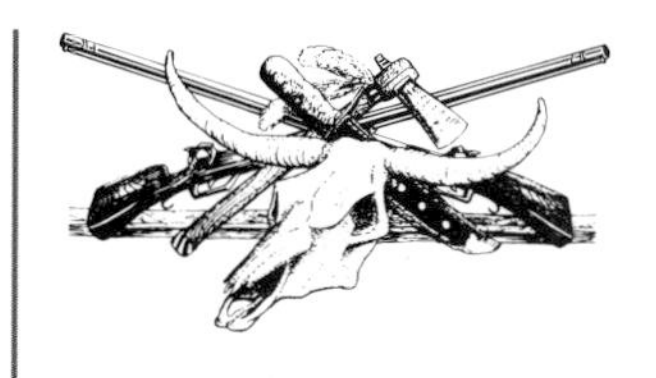

At this point in the journey, Lewis and Clark realized that the "short portage" between the Missouri and a river leading to the Pacific did not exist. But they pushed on, and in October 1805 found the Snake River and followed it into the Columbia, via which, in mid-November, the Corps of Discovery finally reached the Pacific Ocean. They built Fort Clatsop near the present-day state line between Washington and Oregon, spent the winter of 1805–6 there and set off for home in the spring. On the return journey, Lewis continued back along the Missouri, while Clark took a party to explore the Yellowstone River; the two groups met for a triumphant return to St Louis on September 23, 1806.

After their return – and subsequent elevation to the status of living legends – the future held vastly different fates for Meriwether Lewis and William Clark. In 1809, while on his way to Washington to edit the journals of the historic journey he had completed just three years before, Lewis died of pistol wounds mysteriously inflicted in a cabin on Tennes-

**BELOW** Upon reaching the primary objective of their expedition – the Pacific Ocean – Lewis and Clark built Fort Clatsop near the mouth of the Columbia River in Oregon, and spent the winter of 1805–06 there. Nearly 200 years later the outpost still stands.

# MANIFEST DESTINY'S "GREAT PATHFINDER"

**BELOW** The ambitious Captain John Charles Frémont was a gifted Army survivor, promoter and chronicler of the American West, who stimulated westward migration in the 1840s. But both the title "explorer" and the nickname "The Great Pathfinder" were misnomers in Frémont's case. His expeditions were always guided – often by his loyal friend Kit Carson – and he usually followed the trails blazed by others.

During the three decades following the ground-breaking expeditions of Lewis, Clark, Pike and others, the western mountain ranges of North America – including the Rockies, the Sierra Nevada, and others – were penetrated and explored by scores of trappers seeking the fur of abundant beaver and other game. The exploits of the most accomplished of these "mountain men" and scouts – including such legendary personalities as John Colter, Jim Bridger, Jed Smith, Joseph Walker and Kit Carson – were of such importance that our next chapter is devoted to them. However, the discoveries of some of these adventurers were employed, and sometimes exploited, by the expeditions of one of the West's most influential – although ultimately overrated – explorers: John Charles Frémont (1813–90).

Unlike many of the men who explored the West in his day, Frémont – the Georgia-born illegitimate son of a Virginia socialite – was a handsome, college-educated social climber. He combined intellect with skill at making personal connections in a career that began with an appointment to the US Army's Corps of Topographical Engineers in 1838. In that post, Lieutenant Frémont displayed great skill at surveying and map-making. Meanwhile, on the social front, he wooed and (in 1841) secretly married teenaged Jessie Benton – the beautiful daughter of US Senator Thomas Hart Benton, an architect of the expansionist theories of the "Manifest Destiny" of the United States. Although initially opposed to the union and to Frémont, Benton eventually recognized his son-in-law's talents and launched his career as an explorer.

On his first assignment under Benton's sponsorship, between June and October 1842, Frémont led an expedition to map the Oregon Trail as far as the South Pass through the Colorado Rockies. It was the first collaboration between the somewhat reckless Frémont and a soon-to-be-legendary mountain man who would serve as his guide and friend for decades to come – Kit Carson, then 33 years old. The journey itself was not particularly difficult, and even the party's ascent of what came to be known as Frémont's Peak – which Frémont claimed to be the highest in the Rockies, although over 50 were actually taller – was not particularly exciting.

What was remarkable about the expedition, however, was the dazzling report of the journey which Frémont and his wife Jessie composed and which he delivered to Congress the following year. It was a classic piece of propaganda which portrayed a thrilling journey and sang the glories of travelling west; and it launched Frémont's self-promoted image as a living symbol of what a few years later would be called America's "Manifest Destiny" to expand westward.

On his second expedition, carried out in 1843–4, Frémont was supposed to continue the mapping of the Oregon Trail clear to the Pacific, then return eastward along the trail. Instead – after dragging a cannon, against orders, across 3,000 miles of rugged terrain, and getting lost in the mountains more than once – with help from another mountain legend, Joe Walker, Frémont led his party southward from Fort Vancouver into Spanish-held California, eventually returning via a trail blazed a decade earlier by Jed Smith. Once again his detailed report, although it contained such flaws as assuming that

Utah's Great Salt Lake and Utah Lake were one connected body of water, caught the public's imagination and his reputation grew.

But Frémont's greatest adventure – which ultimately led to his undoing – was yet to come. With both Joe Walker and Kit Carson as his guides he set off on an expedition to explore the Great Basin and the Sierras in the summer of 1845. The party of 60 moved along the Arkansas River, across the Continental Divide, through the Rockies, across the Great Basin and through the Sierras into California – which was simmering with rebellion by American settlers against the authority of Mexico, already on the brink of war with the US over disputed territory.

The Mexicans ordered Frémont and his men out of California; initially he refused, then he withdrew to Oregon. But when the Mexican War did break out in 1846, Frémont went back into California, joined forces with rebels there – and then clashed with the victorious American general Stephen Kearny, who accused him of insubordination for apparently attempting to set himself up as governor of the territory. Frémont was court-martialed and dishonorably discharged, but his career was not yet over.

In 1848, with the intention of discovering a transcontinental railroad route through the western mountains, Frémont mounted a brazen midwinter expedition into the Rockies and beyond. Ignoring the advice of his guide, veteran mountain man Bill Williams, Frémont continued on into the San Juan Mountains – where his party was hemmed in by horrible weather. Frémont barely made it out alive in January 1849; 10 other members of the expedition didn't. The undertaking had been a total disaster, but the vain Frémont would never admit it, either to the public or to himself.

And then Frémont's luck changed again. Gold was discovered on a chunk of California land he had purchased by mistake. Great wealth, and a term as one of the first US Senators from the new state of California, followed. In 1856, he was chosen as the first presidential candidate of the newly formed Republican Party, and gave Democratic winner James Buchanan a run for his money. But it was pretty much downhill from there for Frémont. He proved inept as a general during the Civil War, and lost his California fortune to bad business decisions. In his final years he was supported by income from his wife Jessie's writing. Ironically, Frémont died virtually penniless in a New York boarding-house in 1890 – far from the West he had helped to open, in the year in which historians officially declared it closed.

But Frémont's earlier accomplishments, though perhaps greatly inflated by his own ego and much self-promotion, had earned him a lasting place in the history of the American West. Although he was hardly the "Great Pathfinder", John C. Frémont played a pivotal role in drawing thousands of Americans westward to seek their fortunes – and fulfil the nation's "manifest destiny".

**ABOVE** J. C. Frémont's reports of his expeditions, written with his wife Jessie Benton Frémont, were often as grandiose – and as fanciful – as this romantic image of "The Great Pathfinder", claiming a Rocky peak for "God and Country".

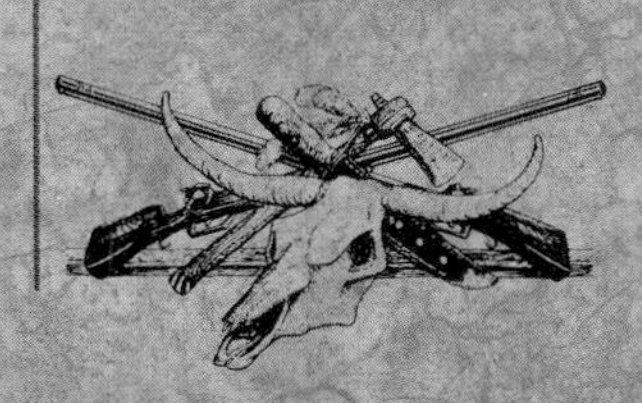

| KEY TO MAP | |
|---|---|
| ■ | fort |
| ● | settlement |
| —— | M. Lewis and W. Clark (1804–06) |
| —— | Zebulon Pike (1805–06) |
| —— | Zebulon Pike (1806–07) |
| —— | Joseph R. Walker (1833–34) |
| —— | John C. Frémont (1842) |
| —— | John C. Frémont (1843–44) |

see's Natchez Trace. The great explorer, only 35, fought death for days; whether he was a victim of murder or a suicide has never been determined. Clark, on the other hand, lived to enjoy a distinguished career in Government service. His remarkable skill in negotiating with Native Americans – who respectfully called him the "red-haired chief" – led to a 30-year stint as the first US Superintendent of Indian Affairs, a post he held until his death in 1838.

Lewis and Clark's Corps of Discovery may not have discovered the legendary "Northwest Passage" – which did not in fact exist – but fulfilled its mission even beyond Jefferson's greatest expectations. The expedition covered and charted nearly 8,000 miles of previously unknown territory. The Corps encountered some 50 Native American tribes, establishing communications with many of them and collecting fine examples of their culture; identified hundreds of new species of plants, birds and animals; added volumes to the nation's existing body of scientific knowledge; and reported observances of game – most notably beaver – which prompted fur trappers to begin the first wave of migration into the territory, effectively "opening" the western half of the continent. The most important expedition in the American West was now history – but America's Western experience was just beginning.

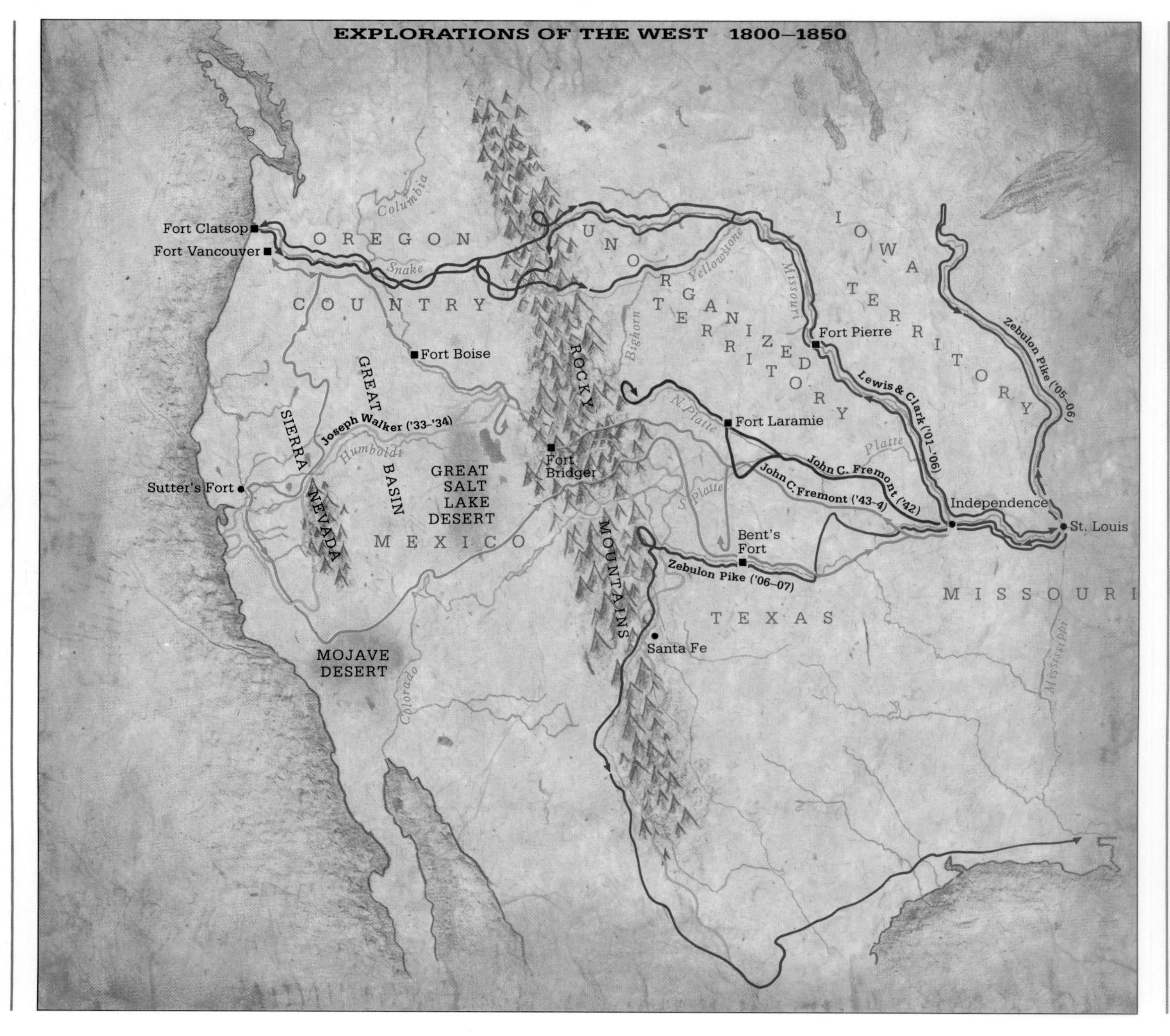

# POWELL EXPLORES THE COLORADO

By 1870, the American West – that vast expanse first explored by Lewis and Clark six decades earlier, and promoted by Frémont just thirty years before – was close to being "conquered". Most of the land between the Mississippi and the Pacific had been surveyed, and much of it had been settled; a transcontinental railroad had been built across it. But a few of the West's more magnificent areas defied exploration since they were deemed too fantastic to be believed, too dangerous or not worth the trouble. These as yet undiscovered regions included such now familiar landmarks as Yellowstone, Yosemite and the Grand Canyon of the Colorado.

During the Civil War, Union officer and Illinois geology professor John Wesley Powell (1834–?) lost one arm to a Confederate bullet. His injury, however, did not stop him from making field trips in the Rockies with his students after the war. One of them inspired him to undertake a voyage in 1869 which no man had ever completed before – to traverse the entire raging Colorado River system by boat, from the Green River in Wyoming to the Virgin River in Nevada.

**LEFT** In 1869, John Wesley Powell, a Civil War hero who had lost an arm at Shiloh, led an expedition of ten men in four small boats down the rapids-filled Colorado and Green rivers. They passed through the entire length of the Grand Canyon and emerged three months later as national heroes.

With a store of surplus Army supplies and three oak boats built with his own money, Powell and a party of nine set off down the Colorado on May 24, 1869. The expedition left civilization behind for some three months, surviving wave after wave of deadly rapids through some of the deepest and most beautiful gorges on Earth – including the incredible Grand Canyon itself. After three members of his party had left to return on foot (and were killed by Indians on their way home), Powell completed the journey on 30 August and returned home to great acclaim. In 1871 he did it again, this time with help from a variety of sources. John Wesley Powell later went on to head the US Geological Survey, but he will always be renowned as the courageous one-armed explorer who dared to challenge the Grand Canyon and the mighty Colorado.

**BELOW** In 1871, John Wesley Powell returned to the Colorado River and the Grand Canyon to continue his explorations – this time with several hundred pounds of bulky photographic equipment. Boatman John K. Hillers took this shot of the expedition's encampment.

# MOUNTAIN MEN AND SCOUTS

A great deal of the post-Lewis-and-Clark exploration of the West carried out between 1810 and 1840 was actually a commercial venture – the search for "beaver water" by fur trappers. These trappers, or "mountain men" as they came to be called, combed the western mountains for rivers and streams teeming with beaver, whose fur was highly sought for use in hats and other fashions of the day. Throughout the 1830s, these intrepid frontiersmen made their precarious living by braving the elements and hostile Indians, ferreting out beaver, trading and blazing trails as they went.

After silk became popular and the fur trade died out in the 1840s, most mountain men became "scouts" – guides for parties of westward-travelling emigrants, explorers or military expeditions whose survival depended upon the skills and knowledge of terrain and Indians that only those with long wilderness experience could possess.

**ABOVE** Incredible as it may seem, much of the great exploration of the vast regions west of the Mississippi, including the Rocky Mountains, between 1820 and 1840, was a direct result of the search for this little critter – the industrious beaver, whose pelts were highly prized as the major component of hats worn by fashionable men of the day.

## The Model Mountain Man: John Colter

One of the earliest trappers to operate in and explore the West was actually a member of Lewis and Clark's Corps of Discovery – a Virginian private named John Colter (*c.*1755–1813) who was granted permission by the captains to leave the expedition on its return trip in 1806 to serve as a guide for two trappers, Forrest Hancock and Joseph Dickson. Although Hancock and Dickson soon retreated from the rigors of mountain life, Colter stayed in the western wilderness for the next three years, often working as a hired guide and trapper for a rather unscrupulous fur trader and outfitter named Manuel Lisa.

Between 1807 and 1810, Colter survived by his wits and extraordinary wilderness skills, exploring many areas of the Rockies where white men had never before trod, usually alone and on foot. During one remarkable solo trek from the junction of the Bighorn and Yellowstone Rivers in the winter of 1807–8, Colter covered a sizeable chunk of what is now Montana, Wyoming and Idaho. He crossed the Continental Divide, the Snake River and the Tetons, and returned with amazing stories of geysers, boiling hot springs and mudpots that he had discovered in the northwest corner of present-day Wyoming. Virtually no one believed him, however, and skeptics dubiously named the area "Colter's Hell". As later travelers would confirm, of course, Colter had indeed been the first white man to witness these natural wonders in what would later become Yellowstone National Park.

During his time in the wilderness, the courageous and resourceful Colter twice thwarted death at the hands of Blackfoot Indians. Once, captured and tortured on the Jefferson River in 1808, he escaped by running naked through miles of thorny canyons, pursued by Blackfeet who believed his claim that he was a slow runner. But after surviving another Blackfoot attack which killed five companions in 1810, Colter called it quits and canoed 2,000 miles down the Missouri to St Louis, where he married and took to farming – only to die of jaundice three years later. Because Colter kept no accurate logs or maps of his journeys he received little credit for his discoveries but his legendary skills and exploits in the West served as the model for a generation of mountain men yet to come.

**BELOW** When mountain men like John Colter and Jim Bridger talked of the amazing natural phenomena they saw in the Yellowstone region – such as the famous Old Faithful Geyser, seen here in a modern photograph of Yellowstone National Park – most people dismissed the reports as trappers' "tall tales".

# Mr Ashley's Rocky Mountain Men

An advertisement placed in an 1822 issue of the St Louis *Missouri Gazette and Public Advertiser* began the careers of a number of mountain men destined to become legends for their wilderness adventures. Placed by William Ashley, the first Lieutenant Governor of the new state of Missouri, the notice sought "enterprising young men" to work as freelance fur trappers in the Western wilderness. Some of the men who answered it (and another like it) later proved among the toughest and ablest trappers and trail-blazers ever to take to the mountains.

They shared the typical life of the mountain man – months of solitary trapping in rugged terrain; constant vigilance to avoid being bushwhacked by hostile Indians; the occasional comforts of an Indian wife; and the release provided by the annual rendezvous – a traditional year-end blow-out, begun by Ashley in 1825, where trappers from all over the Rockies met to sell their pelts, replenish their supplies, drink, fight occasionally, enjoy the favours of local Indian girls and generally carouse before heading back to the lonely mountains. A few of their careers, which began with Ashley's first trapping expedition to the Yellowstone area in the spring of 1823, are recounted here.

## The Beaver Man: Jed Smith

The Bible-toting son of a New Hampshire Methodist family, Jedediah Strong Smith (1799–1831) was 23 when Ashley hired him for his first trapping expedition. In many ways, he was quite unlike most of his fellow trappers – beardless, viceless (he neither drank nor enjoyed the company of women at rendezvous time) and devout. But by the time he was 30 Smith had become the mountain man extraordinaire in the ways that really counted, hauling in the all-time record for beaver pelts in a year (668 in 1825) and blazing trails westward from the Rockies through the Sierras. Although Smith's trails were often stumbled on, many were later followed by

**BELOW** Jed Smith was the first man to conquer the Sierra Nevada from east to west. The range's eastern front, from which this shot of Rock Creek Canyon comes, rises sharply from the Great Basin, while its western slope descends gradually to the hills bordering the central valley of California.

California-bound settlers – making him one of the West's great, if somewhat haphazard, pathfinders.

Smith's accomplishments did not come easy; he survived a mauling by a grizzly, a deadly ambush by Arikara Indians, several tortuous crossings of the Mojave Desert that almost finished off his party, and imprisonment by Spanish authorities for illegally entering their territory. He became, however, the first white man to conquer a number of important crossings: overland from the Rockies to California; east to west through the Sierra Nevada; across Utah's Great Salt Desert; and north from southern California to the Oregon Country. After eight years traversing the West, Smith tried settling down in St Louis in 1830. Restlessness drove him back to the wilderness the following year, this time along the Sante Fe Trail. There Jed Smith's luck finally ran out; while searching for water, he was ambushed and killed by Comanches at the age of 32.

**LEFT** Throughout the 1820s, Jedediah Strong Smith roamed the West as a highly successful, if atypical, mountain man – a pious trapper and trailblazer who never caroused. Following his record-setting 1825 trapping season, Smith bought into the fur company he worked for and in 1826 set off for the South-west in search of beaver water. Instead, he and his party found the Mojave Desert, and barely survived the grueling but historic crossing to California.

**ABOVE** Known to his friends as "Old Gabe", mountain man, guide and scout Jim Bridger (1804–81) enjoyed a long and successful wilderness career. Although he had a way with a tall tale, many of Bridger's least believable reports were actually true – including his "discovery" of the Great Salt Lake while shooting the Bear River rapids, and encountering the wonders of Yellowstone.

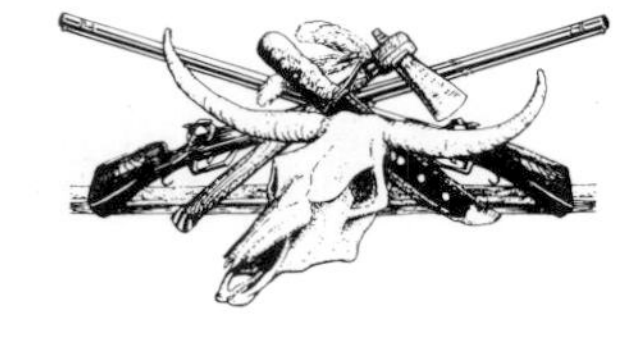

## Trapper, Trader and Trailblazer: Jim Bridger

Only 19 when he joined Ashley's first trapping party into the Rockies in 1823, Jim Bridger (1804–81) was still roaming the mountains over 40 years later. While encamped near the present-day border of Wyoming and Utah in 1825 Bridger took a canoe all the way down the raging Bear River to settle a bet about where it flowed; he ended up in a great body of salt-water. Although at first he believed he had reached an extension of the Pacific, it is generally assumed that Bridger was actually the first white man to discover the Great Salt Lake.

Bridger's wilderness sense and rapport with Indians (he married and survived three successive Indian wives), together with his mapping skills and fluency in Spanish, French and a number of Native American languages, served him well during a long career in the West as an Army scout, "Indian fighter", and expedition guide and supplier, as well as trapper. He set up a fort and trading post on the Oregon Trail in 1843. After the establishment was destroyed a decade later by attacking Mormons, Bridger – now in his 50s – scouted for the Army in the "Mormon War" of 1857. Nearly 10 years later, he was still at it, blazing the Bozeman Trail between Nebraska and Montana, before failing health and eyesight forced his retirement. Leaving many trails – as well as tall tales – behind him, this legendary mountain man died peacefully at the age of 77.

## "Broken Hand": Thomas Fitzpatrick

That first Ashley trapping expedition in 1823 was led by a dashing, fairly well-educated young man named Thomas Fitzpatrick (1799–1854) whose Indian nickname, "Broken Hand", alluded to the three fingers he lost when a rifle exploded in his hands. Like others at the top of his profession, Fitzpatrick survived a long and varied career in the wilderness by developing a great knowledge of and deep respect for Native Americans and their ways. After trapping for Ashley – and surviving such ordeals as the 1832 Battle of Pierre's Hole against the Gros Ventre Indians, which turned his hair prematurely gray and prompted a second Indian nickname, "White Hair", Fitzpatrick formed the Rocky Mountain Fur Company with Jim Bridger and Bill Sublette in the 1830s.

In the 1840s "Broken Hand" became one of the leading wilderness guides of the West, escorting a number of emigrant trains including John C. Frémont's second expedition in 1844 and General Kearny's march to New Mexico during the Mexican War in 1846. Later that year, Fitzpatrick was appointed US Indian Agent for the Arkansas and Platte River areas, and in that post was considered the "one fair agent" by a number of Native American leaders. After negotiating a number of important Indian treaties through the early 1850s which preceded the coming of the reservation system – and surviving three decades on the dangerous frontier – Tom Fitzpatrick died of pneumonia in 1854.

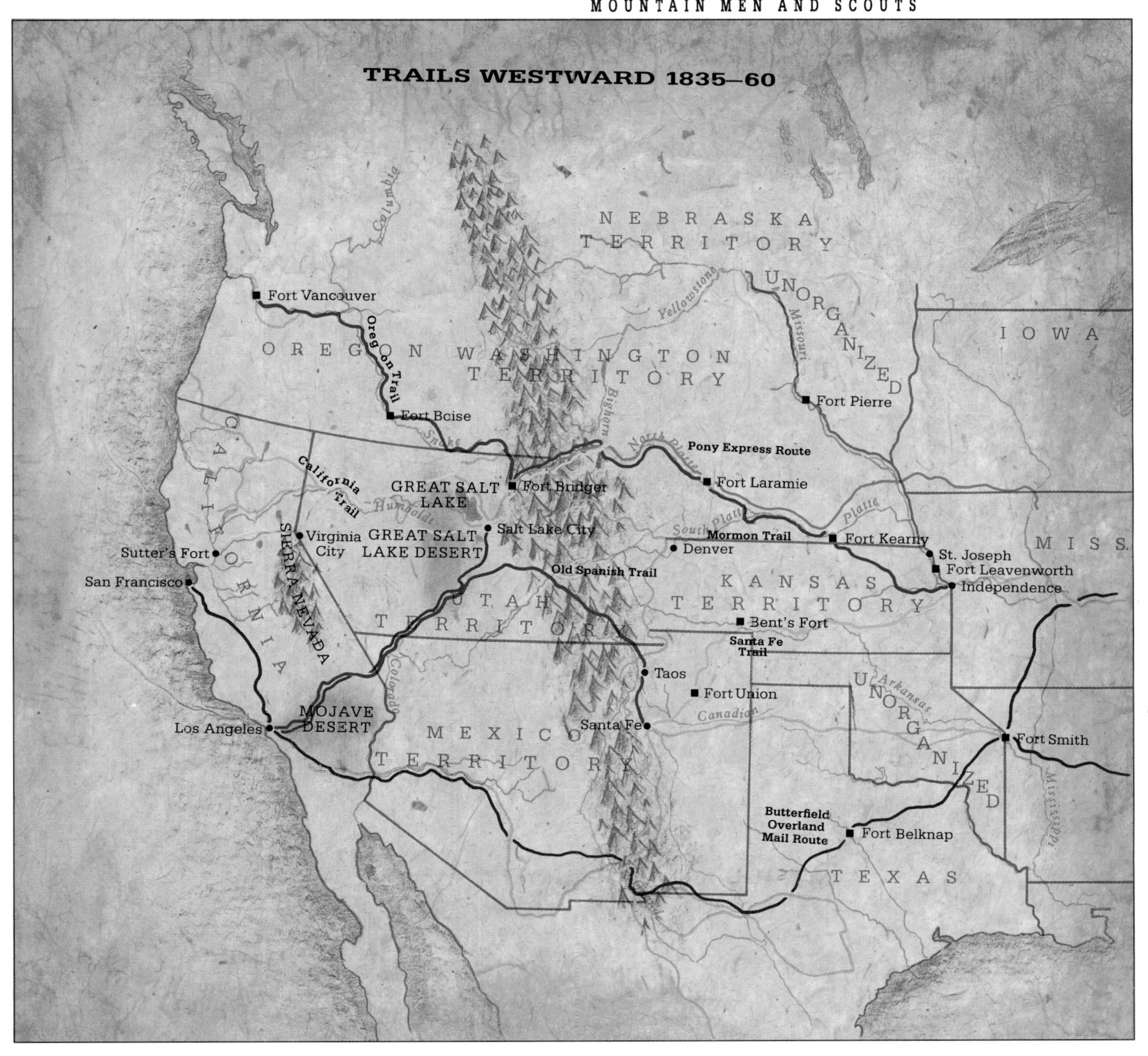


## West with the Mountain Men

Several other members of William Ashley's original Rocky Mountain crew also became well-known veterans of the trapping and scouting trades. William Sublette, a former lawman in St Charles, Missouri, signed on along with his younger brother Milton. Both proved able frontiersmen, and thwarted more than one Indian ambush during their careers. The Sublette brothers joined Fitzpatrick and Bridger as partners in the Rocky Mountain Fur Company; but Billy later left the partnership to strike out on his own as a trader and teamster, supplying trappers and other travelers in the West.

In 1832, Billy guided a party of Oregon-bound settlers organized by businessman Nathaniel Wyeth, from Independence to the annual rendezvous, held that year at Pierre's Hole. Milton then guided the expedition westward – while Billy stayed and took part in a battle in which Gros Ventres attackers faked out the trappers and escaped. Guided by Milton, the Wyeth party reached Fort Vancouver in October; thus, both Sublettes had a hand in escorting the first party of Americans along what would in future be known as the Oregon Trail.

The great danger and adventure experienced by Ashley's mountain men naturally spawned a great many legends. One strange but true tale concerns trapper Hugh Glass, who was mauled by a grizzly while returning to camp during the 1823 expedition. Jim Bridger and another trapper killed the bear, but Glass appeared mortally wounded – so his two companions waited for him to die in

KEY TO MAP

- ■ fort
- ● settlement
- Old Spanish Trail
- Santa Fe Trail
- Oregon Trail
- California Trail
- Mormon Trail

GOVERNMENT POST ROUTES

- Butterfield Overland Mail
- Pony Express

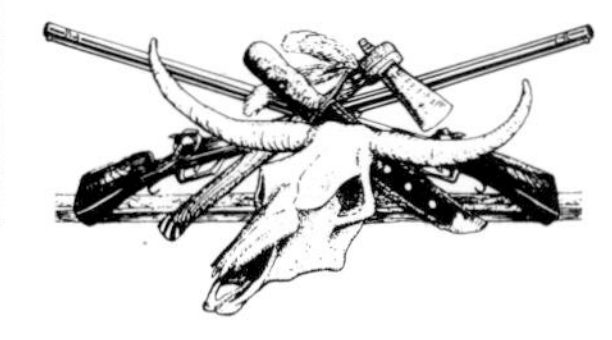

**RIGHT** Sue Beckwourth was among scout Jim Beckwourth's numerous Native American wives. The rugged mulatto mountain man, who particularly cherished the company of Indians and lived with them throughout his life, reportedly took so many Native American brides that he often kept two or more at a time.

**BELOW** Although he excelled in a profession dominated by white men, "mulatto" mountain man/ scout Jim Beckwourth was far more comfortable with Native Americans. The son of a white Southern planter and a black slave, Beckwourth spent much of his life as a Crow – claiming, in fact, to have once been made a chief of that tribe.

order to bury him. Glass hung on for so long, however, that Bridger and the other man simply departed, leaving the "body" on the ground – whereupon Glass literally crawled to the safety of a Sioux encampment and slowly recovered!

James P. Beckwourth (1798–1867), a Virginia-born mulatto whose dark features were often mistaken for those of an Indian, began his wilderness career as a groom with the first Ashley party, but after several years with the trappers turned to those with whom he felt truly at home – Native Americans. Between 1826 and 1833 Beckwourth lived among the Crow, taking several chiefs' daughters as brides and actually becoming a chief himself. He later rejoined white society, scouting for General Kearny during the Mexican War in 1846 and prospecting in the 1859 Colorado gold-rush, before his death in Denver in 1867.

His memoirs, published in 1856, rank among the greatest sources of hogwash and tall tales the West has ever known. One tells how Beckwourth clubbed his disobedient wife – a chief's daughter – and left her for dead. The chief, agreeing that Beckwourth was in the right, presented him with his younger, prettier daughter – only to have the first wife recover and join her sister in the mountain man's household.

Ashley's first 1823 expedition was particularly tough on James Clyman (1791–1881), just beginning a long career as a trapper in the 1820s and 30s, a scout leading wagon-trains to the Pacific coast in the 1840s; and, after 1849, a rancher who lived to the age of 90! On this early occasion, however, the young trapper became separated from his companion Tom Fitzpatrick near the Sweetwater River; Clyman nearly starved to death while walking some 600 miles before reaching sanctuary at Fort Atkinson. But such incidents were almost common in the lives of the mountain men, who contributed greatly to America's westward progress in the first half of the 19th century.

# Trails of the Mountain King: Joe Walker

**ABOVE** Travelers on the Santa Fe Trail from the 1850s onward sought refuge from hostile Indians at Fort Union in present-day New Mexico, seen here from the air.

Although such legendary Western names as Daniel Boone, Davy Crockett, Jed Smith, Kit Carson and others may be more familiar today, another man has been acknowledged by many as perhaps the wisest and greatest – as well as the most romantic – trail-blazer of the American West: Joseph Reddeford Walker (1798–1876). Born on the Tennesse frontier to the family of an early Appalachian settler, Joe Walker set out for the Missouri Territory at the age of 20, following several older brothers who had already headed west. After joining a clandestine – and illegal – trapping and trading expedition to Sante Fe in Spanish territory, the six-foot, 200-lb Walker was transformed into the mountain man personified. Even his own brother, who ran into him on the trail, at first mistook him for an Indian – sporting long hair, a full beard and hunting clothes of ornately beaded buckskin.

In 1825, as part of a US government surveying team, Walker helped establish what would later become the famous Santa Fe Trail. Then, following two terms as Sheriff of Jackson County, Missouri – in which he gained respect as a cool head and a crack shot – Walker signed on in 1832 as field commander for a fur-trapping expedition by an Army captain-on-leave, Benjamin Bonneville. The true purpose of the Bonneville expedition, which yielded little in the way of furs during two years of trapping near the Salmon and Snake Rivers, is still a mystery; some historians believe that Bonneville was conducting Government reconnaissance on British and Spanish possessions, not private enterprise.

## OTHER MOUNTAINS, OTHER MEN

Although many of the legendary mountain men and scouts of the West got their start in the 1820s with William Ashley in the Rockies, a number of legendary wilderness adventurers began their varied careers elsewhere – some of them a generation later.

While grading track – and hunting buffalo – for the Kansas Pacific Railroad, after the Civil War, 21-year-old William Cody allegedly received the nickname "Buffalo Bill" after bringing down 11 of the beasts with 12 shots.

### WILLIAM F. ("BUFFALO BILL") CODY (1846–1917)

During his 72 years, Bill Cody enjoyed one of the greatest careers in Western history. He started early; by the age of 14, he had already worked as a prospector, drover, trapper and Pony Express rider. Like his friend "Wild Bill" Hickok, whom he met during the Civil War, Cody scouted for the Union in its wartime campaign against the Plains tribes, and continued operating against Indians in the service of General Sheridan, General Carr's 5th Cavalry and other commanders after the war.

The dime novels and other popular entertainments of the time had already begun to be filled with rather fanciful accounts of Cody's exploits. His hat – along with a small part of his scalp – was shot off by Cheyennes in 1869 (the same year that Hickok was lanced by the same tribe) in the action leading to a stunning victory over the Cheyenne "Dog Soldiers" at Summit Springs, Kansas.

Shortly thereafter the celebrated scout moved to Fort McPherson, Nebraska, where he inspired dime novelist Ned Buntline to write a serial featuring him and began escorting hunting parties for wealthy men coming west on the newly completed transcontinental railroad. In this capacity Cody guided and entertained government officials, royalty, heads of state, etc., until 1872 when he was recalled to duty. After winning a Congressional Medal of Honor for bravery later that year, Cody left scouting and headed east to begin a theatrical career.

In 1875–6 he returned briefly to scouting in the Sioux Wars where he distinguished himself yet again. From then until his death in 1917, "Buffalo Bill" divided his time between ranching and producing Wild West Shows, which made him wealthy and secured his everlasting fame.

### JAMES BUTLER ("WILD BILL") HICKOK (1837–76)

The dashing, strapping Hickok left his native Illinois at 19 and began his legendary Western career as a lawman in Johnson County, Kansas, in the late 1850s. During the Civil War, "Wild Bill" (the origin of the nickname is unclear) served the Union Army first as a wagon boss and then as a spy, and stories of his courageous exploits began to surface. Scouting against Indians as a civilian for the Army after the war, Hickok cemented his fame as an Indian fighter and the fearless, gunslinging hero of many a dime

**ABOVE** Swashbuckling lawman, scout and Indian fighter, James Butler Hickok, a.k.a. "Wild Bill", began his career as a Union spy. It came to an end some 15 years later with a bullet through the head in a Deadwood saloon.

novel. After a nearly fatal wound from a Cheyenne lance ended his scouting career at 31, Hickok became a lawman again in 1871, adding to his legend as the trigger-happy US marshal who "cleaned up" the tough cow town of Abilene, Kansas. But the cattle trade passed Abilene by in the early '70s, and Wild Bill roamed for a while until settling in Deadwood, a tough mining town in the Black Hills of Dakota – where he was shot to death while playing poker on August 2, 1876, not yet 40. In his renown as a Western hero, "Wild Bill" Hickok is perhaps second only to his close friend "Buffalo Bill" Cody.

### ZENAS LEONARD (1809–1857)

Originally a Pennsylvania farmboy, Leonard headed for St Louis at 21 with the intention of becoming a trapper. Beginning his career in 1831 as a clerk with a trapping expedition in the Rockies, he spent much of the next quarter-century in the wild as a trapper and trader. Leonard recorded his experiences on paper, including the 1832 Battle of Pierre's Hole and Joe Walker's historic 1833 trek to the Pacific, on which he helped blaze the California Trail. His memorable *Narrative* came out in 1839.

### ANTOINE LEROUX (1801–61)

The St Louis-born Leroux did in fact trap briefly for Ashley in 1822, but soon made the Spanish South-west his home, trapping throughout Arizona, New Mexico, Colorado and Utah until the 1840s. Leroux's greatest work came after the Mexican War as scout for the US Army Corps of Topographical Engineers. He blazed trails from Sante Fe to San Diego in 1846–7, from Zuni country to Camp Yuma in 1851, from Missouri to Utah in 1853, and from Fort Smith, Arkansas, to Los Angeles, California, in 1853–4. An old arrow wound contributed to this great pathfinder's death from asthma in 1861.

### JOE MEEK (1810–1875)

A real hell-raiser with a boisterous reputation and a great sense of humor, Meek began trapping at 18 and lived the life of a mountain man until 1840, when he moved his Indian family to the Oregon Country in the first wagon expedition across the Oregon Trail. A great friend of Kit Carson and Jim Bridger, Meek was instrumental in opening Oregon to American settlement, and served the territory as a sheriff, legislative representative, US marshal and commander in the Indian Wars before retiring to his farm there, where he died at 65.

### JAMES OHIO PATTIE (1804–*c*.1850)

A third-generation frontier adventurer, Pattie began accompanying his Jack-of-all-trades father, Sylvester, on wilderness forays from the Missouri region into the Spanish South-west while still a teenager. The pair trapped, mined and trail-blazed throughout the Southwest until jailed by the Mexicans while trying to cross the California desert in 1827. Freed after Sylvester died in jail, James roamed throughout Mexico and California, published an account of his adventures in 1831, and joined the Gold Rush in 1849; he is believed to have died in a Sierra blizzard the following year.

**RIGHT** When a California-bound party led by mountain man *par excellence* Joseph Reddeford Walker crossed the Sierra Nevada, they became the first Anglo-Americans to se the Yosemite Valley in 1833. This was among the breathtaking sights they beheld: the grandeur of Yosemite Falls, whose three "leaps" drop from a total height of 2,425 feet.

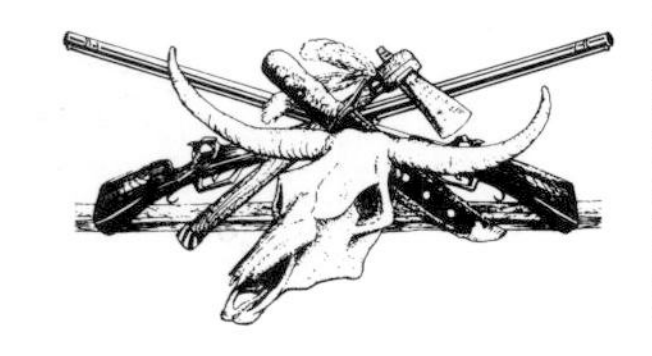

Then, in 1833, Walker organized another Bonneville-sponsored expedition – a seemingly daring trek through the Great Basin and the Sierras to California. But Joe Walker's talents as an intuitive pathfinder, mountain man and leader of men made him – as Zenas Leonard, one of his young recruits and a chronicler of the mountain men, described him, "a man well calculated to undertake a business of this kind."

The Walker party did not take Jedediah Smith's hazardous, rambling route across the Mojave Desert to the Pacific, but followed a carefully planned – and much less dangerous – trail west.

In the summer, Walker's men, well equipped and carrying extra rations, started on horseback through the Great Basin along a path which Walker selected based on information from local Indians and his own intuition. Staying north of the Great Salt Lake and away from the salt deserts to the west, the party moved across the Nevada Plains and along the Humboldt River, fighting off Digger Indians near the Humboldt Sink. In November, after a difficult three-week crossing of the snowy Sierras, Walker's men discovered an incredible sight never before seen by white men – the majestic Yosemite Valley. Finally crossing into California and receiving rest, recreation and a passport from Spanish authorities over the winter, the party was invited to stay and settle. Declining this generous offer, Walker headed east again in the spring of 1834.

On its way back east, the Walker expedition sought and found a less dangerous crossing through the Sierras; known as Walker Pass, it became a favored point of passage for emigrants heading for California. The party arrived back at its Bear River rendezvous point in July 1834, nearly a year after its departure. But the path that Joe Walker had blazed across some of the continent's most dangerous country – to the Pacific and back without a single fatality – became known as the California Trail. It was followed by thousands: first by emigrants, then by prospectors and, 35 years later, by the builders of the Transcontinental Railroad; and the expedition that blazed it sparked enough interest in California to keep settlers coming for years, even before the Gold Rush began.

As for Walker himself, his career was just hitting its stride. He continued trapping and trail-blazing (and at times wenching and carousing) into the 1840s, escorting part of John Frémont's 1845 expedition to California. Even more of an expansionist than Frémont, Walker split with the "Great Pathfinder" when the latter fled to Oregon in 1845, later denouncing Frémont as "morally and physically the most complete coward I ever knew." Well into the 1860s Walker alternated between careers as a wilderness scout and a horse trader, exploring the Colorado River region in 1850, scouting for the Army with Kit Carson in 1859 and leading prospectors to gold in Colorado in 1862 and Arizona in 1863. With his eyesight failing, Joe Walker retired to his nephew's California ranch in 1867, where he died peacefully in the Centennial year of 1876 – perhaps the greatest mountain man and wilderness scout of them all.

**BELOW** Although his name is inexplicably absent from many history books, mountain man Joseph Reddeford Walker – depicted in this 1837 Alfred Jacob Miller painting – was a truly remarkable figure in the exploration of the West. The handsome six-footer could find a path, seek out water or lead an expedition better than anyone.

## KIT CARSON: THE CONSUMMATE FRONTIER SCOUT

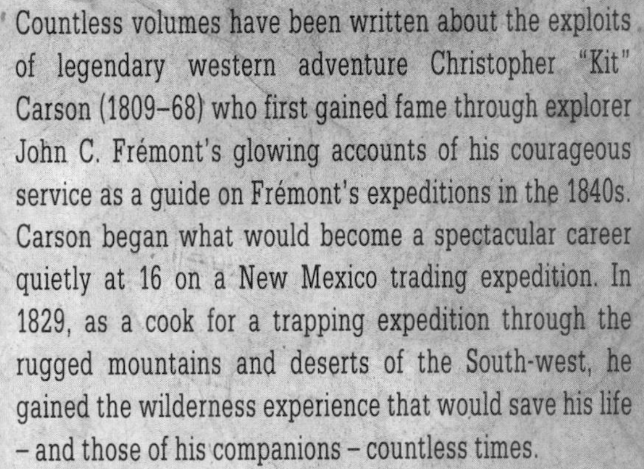

**RIGHT** Christopher "Kit" Carson gained national fame after guiding John C. Frémont's highly publicized Western explorations in the 1840s.

**BELOW** The majestic, forbidding cliffs of Canyon de Chelly in Arizona Territory failed to thwart Kit Carson's decisive 1864 victory over the Navajo.

Countless volumes have been written about the exploits of legendary western adventure Christopher "Kit" Carson (1809–68) who first gained fame through explorer John C. Frémont's glowing accounts of his courageous service as a guide on Frémont's expeditions in the 1840s. Carson began what would become a spectacular career quietly at 16 on a New Mexico trading expedition. In 1829, as a cook for a trapping expedition through the rugged mountains and deserts of the South-west, he gained the wilderness experience that would save his life – and those of his companions – countless times.

He trapped throughout the 1830s, and in the '40s began signing on to various expeditions in every corner of the West as a freelance scout and Indian fighter. As Carson's legend grew over the years through factual reports and dime novels, so did his image as a big, strapping, dashing mountain man – while in fact he was slight, soft-spoken and almost shy. Carson, who was illiterate but could speak Spanish, French and Indian languages, had a keen intelligence that led him to approach his dangerous work very professionally, leaving nothing to chance.

After scouting for the Army in the Mexican War, trying his hand at farming and serving as an Indian agent through the 1850s, Carson received an Army commission when the Civil War broke out in 1861. While the fighting that raged between the states in the East occupied the Federal troops who once kept the Indians in check, Carson operated in the West. Placed in command of a volunteer army, the veteran scout was charged with subduing the bands of Navajos, Apaches, Kiowas and Comanches that had been terrorizing the South-west since the start of the war. Carson's reputation as an Indian fighter soared as he first starved the Navajos out of their New Mexico strongholds in 1863, then defeated them in Arizona's Canyon de Chelly and at Adobe Walls in Texas – routing some 3,000 Indians with only 400 troops – the following year. By the war's end, Carson had risen to the rank of Brigadier-General – the only illiterate one in the US Army. In 1868, at the age of 59, after surviving nearly 45 years in the Wild West, Kit Carson met an unlikely death from injuries sustained in a hunting accident at Fort Lyon, New Mexico.

PART II

# WESTWARD, HO!

Following the trails blazed through the Western wilderness by the explorers and mountain men during the first four decades of the 19th century, a steady stream of emigrants began to flow westward in the 1840s. Incredibly, within the next 50 years most of the "free land" west of the Mississippi would be claimed, and America's western frontier would be declared officially "closed". But the actual "push" westward between the 1840s and the Civil War years produced many stories and legends that are well worth the telling.

# SODBUSTERS, TEXANS AND 49ERS

**BELOW** In this contemporary view of Salt Lake City in 1853, six years after its settlement, the Mormon desert community sits squarely in the shadow of the Wasatch Mountains. Brigham Young had once envisaged Salt Lake City as the capital of the independent Mormon state of Deseret; that dream was not to be, but the city did become the capital of the predominantly Mormon state of Utah.

Spurred on by glowing reports of the West's bounty by such explorers as J.C. Frémont, thousands of settlers braved the dangers of the wilderness in the 1840s and '50s to begin new lives as farmers on the vast plains west of the Mississippi – to become "sodbusters", carving farms out of the prairie sod. Even earlier – since the 1820s, in fact – Americans had been settling in Texas, and in the 1830s they rebelled against Mexican constitutional rule, becoming a republic until they won entry into the United States in 1845.

Following the Mexican War in 1846, the former Mexican possessions of New Mexico and California – where a gold-rush ensued in 1849 – became American territory, as well. Territorially, at least, the US we know today had largely taken shape by 1850, but settling this great new land would prove to be an adventure for the age.

# The Odyssey of the Mormons

**BELOW** The epitome of the filthy shantytown that boomed into a thriving mining "city" virtually overnight, Virginia City, Nevada, sprung up after the 1859 discovery of unusually rich gold and silver ore in the Comstock Lode. The town, seen in this 1868 photo by Tim O'Sullivan, was named after one of lucky prospector Henry Comstock's original partners – James "Old Virginny" Finney, who sold his interest in Comstock's mine for a blind horse and a bottle of whiskey.

Since its establishment in New York State in 1830, the Church of Jesus Christ of Latter-day Saints – the Mormon Church – had been looking for its Promised Land, its "Zion". The Church's prophet and founder, Joseph Smith (1805–44), had led his Mormon followers through a series of communities in which they established successful settlements, only to be driven away by the hostility of non-Mormons, or "Gentiles" as the "Saints" called them: Kirtland, Ohio (1831–3); Independence, Missouri (1833–8), and the town they built themselves on the Mississippi – Nauvoo, Illinois, in 1838.

At Nauvoo, the wealth generated by the devout, hardworking Mormons' thriving communal theocracy – along with widespread rumors of Joseph Smith's unacknowledged practice of polygamy – earned the Saints the growing resentment of their neighbors in the early 1840s. Incensed by the criticism of a newspaper published by Mormon dissenters within his own community, Smith declared his own martial law in Nauvoo and destroyed the paper's press. Charged with violating the Constitution, Smith and several

**RIGHT** Emerging as the leader of the Mormon Church following the 1844 murder of its founder Joseph Smith, Brigham Young beat incredible odds by keeping his Latter-Day Saints together on a grueling two-year journey that ended near the shores of the Great Salt Lake in 1847.

of his elders were jailed in Carthage, Illinois, in June 1844. On the 27th, Joseph Smith and his brother Hyrum were murdered by a lynch mob of disguised Illinois militiamen at the jail in Carthage.

A 43-year-old Mormon elder named Brigham Young (1801–77) emerged to lead the Saints out of Illinois following Smith's death. Young, a pragmatic Vermonter with a flair for organization, decided by mid-1845 to lead his flock – which now numbered nearly 20,000 – across the plains and through the Rockies to a Promised Land where the Saints could live undisturbed and free from persecution. Just where their Zion was Young was not certain, but he considered the valley of the Great Salt Lake a possibility after reading J.C. Frémont's report on the region. In any case, he claimed, he would know it when he saw it.

Beginning in February 1846, the Mormons journeyed from Nauvoo, across the Mississippi and into Iowa. Nearly 16,000 Saints, traveling in small wagon-trains which stopped to harvest and replant plots of land which the previous group had sown, made their way to a spot near present-day Omaha, Nebraska. There Young established winter quarters to wait out the harsh winter of 1846–7, during which some 700 Mormons died of exposure and illness. Moving on in the early spring of 1847, the faithful journeyed along the North Platte through Nebraska, ever vigilant for Indian attacks. Stopping at Fort Laramie and Fort Bridger, Young was warned – by legendary mountain man Jim Bridger himself – that settling in the Great Salt Lake area was not wise. Nevertheless, the thousands of Saints pushed on through the spring and crossed through the South Pass – and the Continental Divide – on June 27, 1847, three years to the day after the murder of their founder Joseph Smith. On July 24, Brigham Young, seriously ill with fever, saw the valley of the Great Salt Lake for the first time, and declared that his people had arrived – the "Mormon Trail" had reached its destination.

The Mormon emigrants planted crops in the sun-baked earth almost immediately, but they were slow in taking. There was little vegetation, and the bleakness of the place caused many Saints to wonder if they had indeed found their Zion. But eventually the crops – and the settlement itself – took root. The first crops were nearly destroyed by crickets and grasshoppers, who were eaten by flocks of seagulls just in time.

**BELOW** Faced with bleak desert landscapes like this one, where nothing but cactus seemed to grow, the Mormon settlers of Utah persevered, irrigated the land and finally made the desert bloom.

After the first harvest that summer of 1847, Young headed east again to organize further Mormon migration, later returning to the settlement to plan and build his Zion – Salt Lake City. That frontier metropolis became the capital of what Brigham Young had hoped would become an independent Mormon state called Deseret, extending north into Oregon and Washington, east to Kansas, south into New Mexico and even encompassing part of southern California to the west. Throughout those early years the settlement suffered through harsh winters, however the industrious Mormons persevered, irrigating their fertile but arid land and making it yield; eventually their Zion thrived. With the Gold Rush in 1849, the Saints prospered from the commerce generated by the swarms of prospectors who stopped and traded with them. But the Mormon state of Deseret would not come to pass; the area was made a US Territory in 1850, and later entered the Union as Utah, with Young as Territorial Governor.

As more "Gentile" emigrants passed through Utah in the 1850s, Young faced further threats to the Saints, including an 1857 clash with the US Government. He was replaced as Territorial Governor, and US President James Buchanan sent troops marching into Salt Lake City in what came to be called the "Mormon War". Young and his followers evacuated the city and prepared to burn it down if the troops stopped and encamped there; they didn't, and further "war" was averted. Although no longer the governor of the territory he had founded and built, Brigham Young remained an influential leader in his Zion for another 20 years until his death in 1877. Salt Lake City stands today as a modern metropolis that began with an incredible westward trek by a remarkable people, along the "Mormon Trail".

**LEFT** In a long search for its "Zion", or "Promised Land", the Church of Jesus Christ of Latter-Day Saints – the Mormons – carried on an almost constant westward migration between 1830 and 1847, when Brigham Young led his "Saints" to finally settle in the forbidding country around Utah's Great Salt Lake. For decades to come, saints flocked to their Zion in the desert, as evidenced by this photo of a Mormon wagon train moving westward in 1879.

**BELOW** On April 6, 1892 – nearly 40 years after it was begun, and 15 years after Brigham Young's death – the capstone was laid on the six-spired granite Mormon Temple built by the Church of Jesus Christ of Latter-Day Saints in Salt Lake City, Utah.

# The Emigrants

Even before gold was discovered in California in 1848, hundreds of pioneers had endeavoured to cross the continent to start a new life on the Pacific Coast. The stories of two particular emigrant parties to California – one travelling in 1841, the other five years later – illustrate the triumph and the tragedy of the great trek westward.

## California, Here We Come: The Bidwell–Bartleson Party

Although neither of its two young leaders had any experience in moving a wagon-train through the western wilderness, the party of John Bidwell and John Bartleson set off to California via the Oregon trail in the spring of 1841. Early on, the group of 69 men, women and children had the good fortune to hook up with a party of Jesuits guided by the legendary mountain man and scout Tom "Broken Hand" Fitzpatrick. They traveled over a thousand miles under Broken Hand's direction until reaching Soda Springs in Oregon Country, where half of the party decided to head for Oregon. But the 34 others – now without Fitzpatrick's guidance – continued on to California, despite trappers' advice not to try to take wagons through the Sierras.

So on the party went. As the terrain grew more formidable, they were forced to abandon their wagons one at a time. After stumbling through the Great Salt Lake Desert, they happened upon Mary's River, which would later be named the Humboldt by J.C. Frémont. The Bidwell–Bartleson party followed the river to its sink, then continued along what came to be known as Walker River to the foothills of the Sierra Nevada – and in so doing followed roughly the same trail that Joe Walker had blazed nearly a decade earlier. After struggling across the Sierras, reduced to killing their oxen for food lest they starve, the emigrants reached the San Joaquin Valley in late October, some six months since beginning their journey. They then headed for the ranch of Bidwell's friend John Marsh, the California settler whose glowing reports of the country had drawn Bidwell to undertake his journey in the first place. They had arrived – and their successful crossing inspired hundreds more to head to California over the same trail. But not all of these subsequent migrants were as lucky as Bartleson and Bidwell.

**RIGHT** Bearing mute testimony to the hundreds of hardy westward emigrants who made them, the ruts of wagon wheels still mark a section of the Oregon Trail in Wyoming – a century-and-a-half after the Bidwell–Bartleson party followed the trail on the first successful crossing in California by wagon.

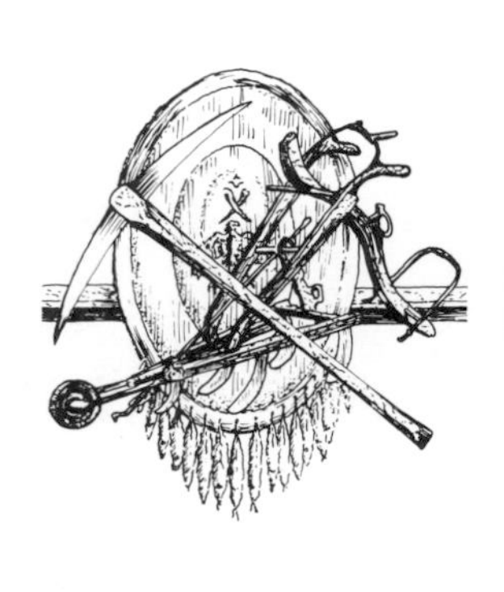

## Tragedy on the Trail: The Donner Party

In 1844–5, nearly four years after the Bidwell–Bartleson party stumbled into California, a blacksmith named Elisha Stephens led the first wagon-train to successfully cross the Sierras. His party was guided by mountain man Caleb Greenwood, who subsequently led several other wagon-trains into California along the tracks left by the Stephens party. Such successes made many prospective emigrants a bit less wary of the dangers of crossing the mountains with loaded wagons; such a group was the unfortunate Donner party.

The families of prosperous farmers George and Jacob Donner, furniture manufacturer James Reed and others formed a large westbound party in Independence, Missouri, and set out for California in May 1846. Their wagons were large and laden with all sorts of comforts – Reed's even had a bar stocked with liquor – and proceeded to the Wyoming country with little trouble. Indeed, much of the Donner party's crossing of the plains was typical of the "sodbuster's" journey; the journal of George Donner's daughter Eliza describes scenes of the pioneer women quilting as the wagons rolled along and their children riding with the "wild, free spirit of the plain".

Trouble, however, was just ahead for these emigrants. Upon reaching Fort Bridger the huge group split up, and the Donners decided to take their party of 87 through the Hastings Cutoff – a "short cut" running south of the Great Salt Lake – instead of north to Fort Hall and along the established California Trail.

**ABOVE** Since mountain man Jim Bridger accidentally floated into its saline waters, Utah's Great Salt Lake and its environs have figured in the "taming" of the West. In the 1820s, Jed Smith nearly died trying to cross the desert south of it; in 1846, most of the Donner emigrant party did die (in the Sierras) after taking a "shortcut" around it; the following year, Brigham Young's Mormons found their Promised Land near its shores; and in 1869, the Transcontinental Railroad was completed at Promontory Point – from which this photo was taken.

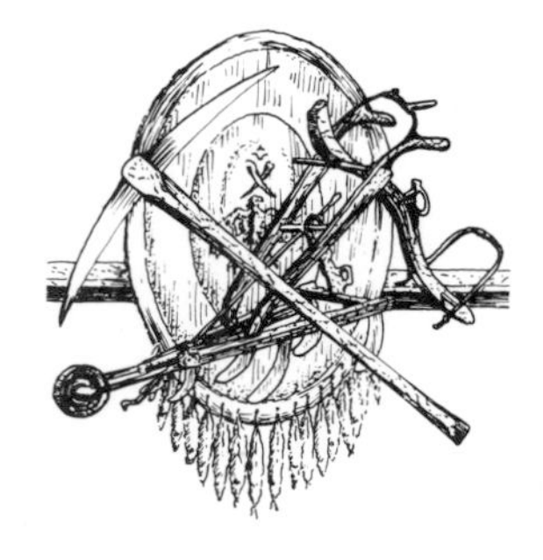

This route, as it turned out, was so much more difficult that it slowed the party's progress down considerably – and it only reached the Sierras in October, with winter closing in.

East of Truckee Pass in the Sierras, the Donner party was forced to dig in for the winter – and they were promptly hemmed in by terrible snowstorms. Their provisions eventually gave out, and although Reed and others managed to get back to civilization and return with rescue parties, it was too late. Many of the emigrants had already starved to death; those who survived did so only by consuming the flesh of their fallen comrades. One survivor, a German immigrant named Lewis Keseberg, reportedly continued eating human flesh after oxen meat was dug up from the snow. Years later, Keseberg denied accusations that he had killed George Donner's wife Tamsen, replying, "There were plenty of corpses lying around."

The Donner disaster tragically pointed out that crossing the Western wilderness was still dangerous business. Only 47 of the 81 emigrants who dug in for the winter near Truckee Pass – later renamed Donner Pass in memory of the victims – survived to reach California. Interestingly, once they had recovered from their ordeal, many of the Donner survivors continued to encourage friends and relatives back home to come out west – provided that they be sure to, "Never take no cut ofs [cutoffs] and hury [hurry] along as fast as you can", as John Reed's daughter Virginia advised a cousin back east.

**BELOW** Emigrant families in covered wagons cross the plains and enter the Rocky mountains. The account of the Donner party's tragic encounter with the terrain stands in bleak contrast to this idealized vision of the trek West, published by Currier and Ives in 1866.

## MOVERS AND SHAKERS OF THE WESTWARD MIGRATION

As the "prairie schooners" rolled out over the North American plains in the mid-1800s, carrying sodbusters to their new ranches in the Great West, a number of men ranging from merchants to missionaries, from politicians to plowmakers, played important roles in the "Great Migration". Here are brief glimpses of a few of them.

### THOMAS HART BENTON (1782-1858)

For three decades, Benton served the cause of what would be called America's "Manifest Destiny" while representing the state of Missouri in the US Senate. Although he didn't coin the term, Benton certainly championed what it stood for – the right of the United States to expand its territory westward. To that end – first as a St Louis Journalist and later (from 1820–50) as a Senator, Benton supported a variety of policies designed to foster that expansion (although early on he envisioned the Rockies as the natural border of the US): the establishment of an overland trail to the California and Oregon coasts; the early US annexation of Texas; opportunities for poor Eastern farmers to thrive in the West, and exploration of the uncharted Western wilderness (by his son-in-law, John C. Frémont). He did, however, oppose the Mexican War and the extension of slavery into new territories, and this lost him his Senate seat in 1850.

JOHN DEERE (1804–86)

The man who invented "the plow that broke the plains" was a Vermont farmboy who set up shop as a blacksmith in Grand Detour, Illinois in the 1830s. Since the cast-iron plow used at the time proved ineffective on the tough, sticky prairie sod, Deere and his partner Leonard Andrus fashioned one with a self-polishing steel plowshare in 1838. The "Grand Detour Plow" was dubbed the "singing plow" because of the ease with which it scoured. It not only proved that the prairie could be farmed – thereby "opening" the vast plains to the "sodbusters" – but the great demand for it also helped foster the American steel industry. In 1846 Deere opened a farm-machinery factory in Moline, Illinois, and the successful company it spawned still bears his name today.

**FAR LEFT** Before losing his Senate seat in 1850, Missouri's Thomas Hart Benton was among the most powerful expansionists in the US Government.

**LEFT** Farm machinery used throughout the United States bears the name of John Deere, an Illinois blacksmith, whose revolutionary steel plow "broke the plains" of the West.

**ABOVE** Aaron Montgomery Ward, the orginator of the mail-order catalogue and supplier of goods to the "sodbusters".

## AARON MONTGOMERY WARD (?-1913)

Just a child when the first great western migrations took place, Ward played an influential role in the lives of the next generation of sodbusters. A retail clerk in a Chicago dry-goods store in 1871, he soon began a business of his own – selling goods to farmers and others in rural areas through "mail-order" at discount prices. Although he lost his initial inventory in Chicago's "Great Fire" later that year, he soon went back into business as Montgomery Ward & Co. and published his first catalogue in 1872. As the sole source of goods for many farm families across the plains, Ward's company continued to be an expanding concern even after the "closing" of the American West in 1890 and his death in 1913.

## DR JOHN MCLOUGHLIN

Born in Quebec, this formidable, white-haired fur trader was appointed chief factor of the Columbia watershed for Britain's Hudson Bay Company in 1824. In that position, McLoughlin controlled most of the Oregon Country from his headquarters at Fort Vancouver, between 1824 and 1846. Although an able protector of his company's interests, McLoughlin often aided emigrants to the Oregon Country, including Americans – even if their intentions were suspect. In 1834, he helped the Boston expansionist Hall Jackson Kelley recover from malaria, lending him money to return east, and he assisted missionaries Jason Lee and Marcus Whitman in establishing settlements in Oregon in the 1830s and '40s.

### DR MARCUS WHITMAN (1800–47)

A devout Congregationalist physician from upstate New York, Whitman led a party of men and women – the first white women to cross the continent (including his wife, Narcissa, whom he married on the trail) – to establish a mission in Oregon in 1836. During the difficult crossing, Whitman tried unsuccessfully to prove that wagons could make it over the Oregon Trail. But the emigrants themselves did make it, and established a mission deep in the Oregon wilderness (near today's Walla Walla, WA) with help from Hudson Bay Company's John McLoughlin.

Over the next decade the settlement grew, and Whitman became a leading voice for emigration to the Oregon Country. In 1843, after a trip back east, he helped lead the first wagon-train to the Pacific. Incoming settlers, however, brought along diseases such as measles that killed hundreds of local Cayuse Indians in the late 1840s. Suspecting Whitman of saving only his own people, several angry Cayuse attacked his mission on November 29, 1847, killing the physician, his wife and 11 others, and prompting an appeal for US Government help.

**BELOW** In 1843, missionary Dr Marcus Whitman led the first emigrant train to his mission in the Oregon country; he was murdered there in 1847.

# The Texans

## The "Father" of The Lone Star State: Stephen F. Austin

Between 1800 and 1820, no less than three expeditions were launched into Spanish-controlled Texas by American adventurers intent on establishing a new territory; each of them failed. But in 1820, a Missouri merchant and mine-owner named Moses Austin (?–1821) asked for Spanish authorities to grant him permission to establish a colony with some 300 American (and Roman Catholic) families. The Spaniards agreed, and Austin returned to Missouri in 1821 to round up the emigrants for the venture. Unfortunately, he came down with pneumonia and died before he could organize the trip back to Texas.

It was Moses Austin's last wish that his oldest son carry out his dream. A well-educated and resourceful young man, Stephen F. Austin (1793–1836) grew up among French and Spanish settlers in what was then Spanish Missouri and attended prep. school in Connecticut and university in Kentucky. He had already worked managing his father's mines and in banking, and even served as a legislator and a circuit judge. Now, at 28, Stephen left further law studies and journeyed to Texas to found the colony with the "Old 300" families as his father had planned.

Austin's first "Texians" built a settlement in the fertile valley of the Colorado and Brazos Rivers – land equally good for growing cotton or corn and for raising livestock. Aside from thwarting repeated Indian interference, the colony faced its first real challenge in 1822 when the new Mexican Government – which had won its independence from Spain the year before – hedged over honoring the Texans' land grant. After traveling to Mexico

**BELOW** Between 1821 and 1836, Stephen Fuller Austin, who had served as an attorney and legislator, led the growth of Texas from a small colony of Americans to an independent state.

**LEFT** In this idealized scene, Texas founder Stephen Austin reaches for his rifle in response to reports of a raid by hostile Indians.

City, and waiting over a year before the political turmoil that accompanied Mexican independence died down, Austin finally saw his grant confirmed in 1823. Later that year the Texans planned and built their log-cabin capital, San Felipe de Austin, on the banks of the Brazos.

Under Austin's leadership, Texas grew and prospered, and the satisfied Mexican Government actually encouraged immigration from the States to Texas. By 1827, an American-born population that had begun with the "Old 300" had mushroomed to 10,000 – and to 20,000 by 1830. Although Austin himself strove to maintain Texas's loyalty to the Mexican Government, the ever-growing American-born population increasingly resented Mexican rule – while the Mexicans themselves began to worry about the Americans taking over. And within one year of refusing US President Andrew Jackson's attempt to purchase Texas for $5 million, the Mexican Government began moving troops into the area to keep the settlers in check.

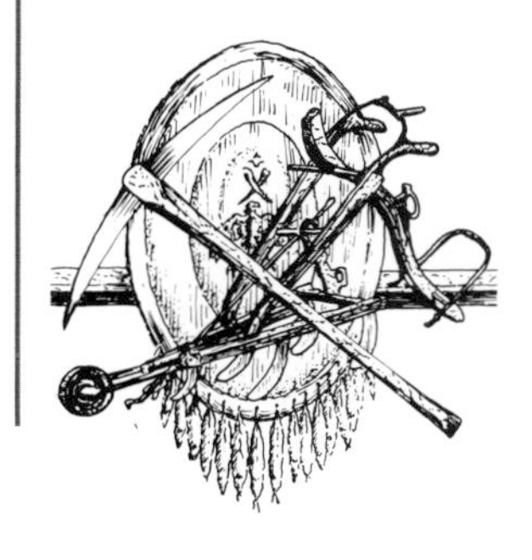

**RIGHT** The self-styled "Napoleon of the West", Mexican General D. Antonio Lopez de Santa Anna, ruled as dictator of the Republic of Mexico at the time of his ruthless victory at the Alamo in 1835.

## The Texas Revolution

Between 1830 and 1835, the Anglo-American population of Texas grew to 30,000, and the territory simmered with unrest. Mexico's policies toward Texas appeared to soften somewhat in 1832, when General Antonio Lopez de Santa Anna (1794–1876) took control of the Government, but his subsequent rise to dictator brought him into direct conflict with the Texans. Austin, who met with Santa Anna in Mexico City in November 1833, was arrested while returning to Texas. By the time he was released in 1835, relations had strained to the breaking-point; on October 2, 1835 the Texas Revolution began.

## Houston Leads the Way

One of the thousands of settlers who moved to Texas between 1830 and 1835 was a man in the middle of an extraordinary career – who had already served as the governor of one state – Sam Houston (1793–1863). A soldier's son and lifelong adventurer who began

**RIGHT** A born soldier and able statesman, Sam Houston spearheaded Texas's military drive for independence in 1835–36, and as President guided the new republic through most of its nine-year history as a sovereign state. In 1845, just as the wily Houston had planned, President Tyler and the US Congress fell for a bluff that Britain was extremely interested in the republic, and moved to create the "Lone Star State".

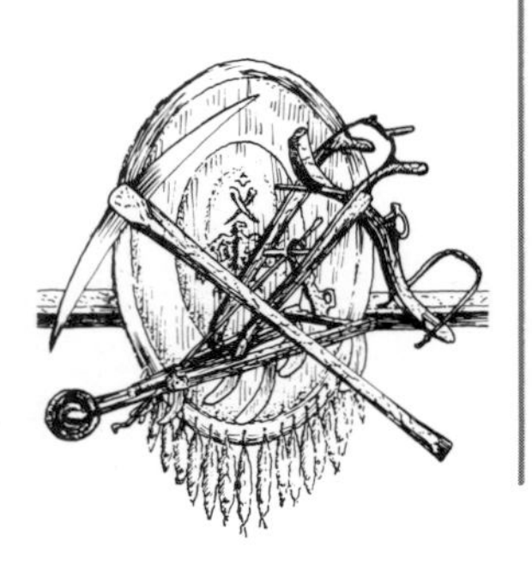

his military career with distinguished infantry service under Andrew Jackson against the Creeks at the Battle of Horseshoe Bend in 1814, Houston had lived for years among the Cherokees in Tennessee. After Horseshoe Bend, he worked briefly for the Indian Bureau (but resigned after being reprimanded for wearing Indian buckskins in Washington), studied law in Nashville, and used the patronage of his old commander, Andrew Jackson, to begin a political career. He was elected to Congress in 1823, and became Governor of Tennessee in 1827 – only to resign in scandal when his young wife left him, presumably because of his drinking and womanizing.

Returning to the Cherokees, Houston became a spokesman for the Cherokee nation and other tribes, and in this capacity headed to Texas in 1832. When the trouble with Mexico began, Houston was the logical choice to lead the Texans' military organization, and was named commander-in-chief in November 1835 by Austin and other members of a ruling committee. Throughout the struggle for independence Houston's forces were always small, but he kept moving and took every advantage he could in the face of Santa Anna's vastly superior numbers.

On March 2, 1836, Austin, Houston and some 57 other leaders gathered to sign Texas' Declaration of Independence. Just four days later, a 13-day siege of the Alamo mission near San Antonio ended when all of its 182 defenders were killed in an attack by some 6,000 Mexicans under Santa Anna. Houston's troops retreated to the east, and the Texas Government itself fled to Galveston Island. On the 20th of that month, a force of 350 Texans was captured near Goliad; a week later, Santa Anna ordered all of the prisoners shot. These defeats, combined with Houston's constant retreats – and rumours of his drinking problem – made the Texans' defeat seem a certainty.

**BELOW** A view of the damaged Alamo mission in San Antonio, Texas, in 1845, nearly a decade after the fatal attack which killed 182 defenders and spurred the Texas Army on to victory – and ultimately independence – one month later at San Jacinto.

But "Old Sam" bided his time and maneuvered behind Santa Anna's overconfident troops encamped near the San Jacinto River in April. On April 21, 1836 an expected dawn attack by the Texans did not come, and Santa Anna ordered his troops to take a rest. When they did, Houston struck, his volunteers shouting, "Remember the Alamo!" At a cost of only 9 dead and 34 wounded, Houston's Texans destroyed Santa Anna's force of nearly 1,400 – killing 630 and capturing more than 700. In 18 minutes the war for Texas independence was won at San Jacinto.

Tragically, only a few months after the San Jacinto victory that allowed Texas to become a republic, the founder of that republic was gone. The struggle of the last 15 years finally caught up with Stephen Austin, who died on December 27, 1836 at the age of 43. Meanwhile Sam Houston had been sworn in as the first President of the Republic of Texas in October, a post he held until 1838, and again from 1841 to 1844.

**ABOVE** This unidentified Texas Ranger, mounted and ready for action, was typical of the lawmen who tracked down and brought in countless rustlers and gunslingers throughout the West between the 1860s and 1900.

**RIGHT** As Sam Houston's political rival and successor as President of the Republic of Texas, Mirabeau Buonaparte Lamar championed the continued independence of Texas and opposed annexation by the US. In an attempt to foster trade and strengthen Texas's territory and treasury, Lamar launched an ill-advised invasion of New Mexico in 1841. It failed, nearly ruining the young republic, and ended Lamar's career.

Throughout this period, Houston's chief political adversaries were Mirabeau B. Lamar, a poet and musician who advocated continued Texas independence, and David G. Burnet, who had been Provisional President during the war. Lamar succeeded Houston in the Presidency between 1838 and 1841 and moved the capital to Austin, but his career ended in 1841 when the Mexicans captured an ill-conceived Texan invasion force in New Mexico. Houston, who regained the Presidency later that year, held it until 1844, always pushing for US statehood – which was granted to Texas in 1845 as a slave state. Upon the Lone Star State's admission to the Union, "Old Sam" served in the US Senate for 13 years (1846–59), then became Governor until 1861. Since he opposed both slavery and secession, Houston refused to take the Confederate oath when the Texan legislature voted to secede, and was removed from office. The legendary leader then retired to his wife and eight children on his Alabama farm, and died of pneumonia on July 26, 1863 – reportedly calling the names of what may have mattered to him most in life: his wife Margaret, and Texas.

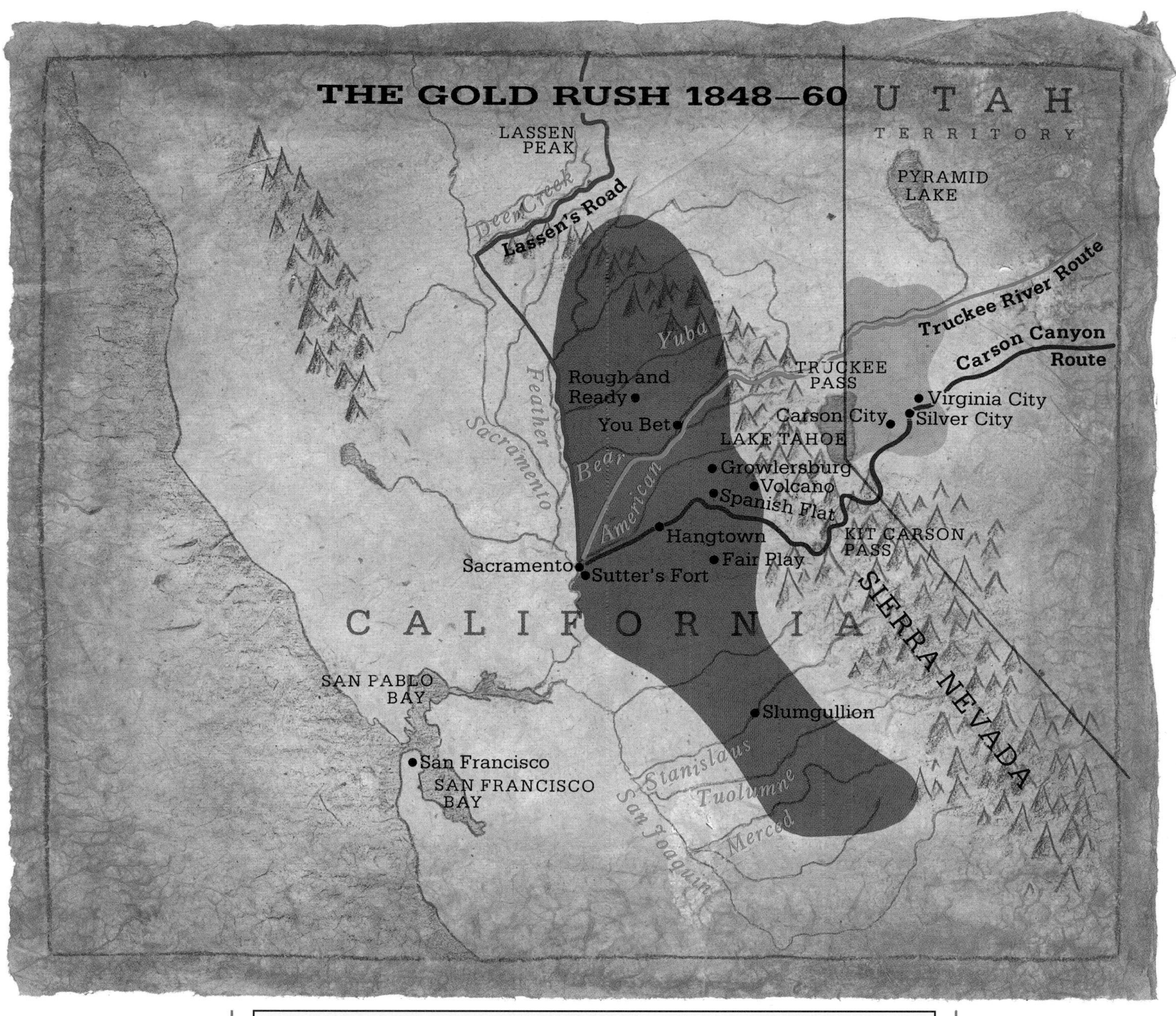


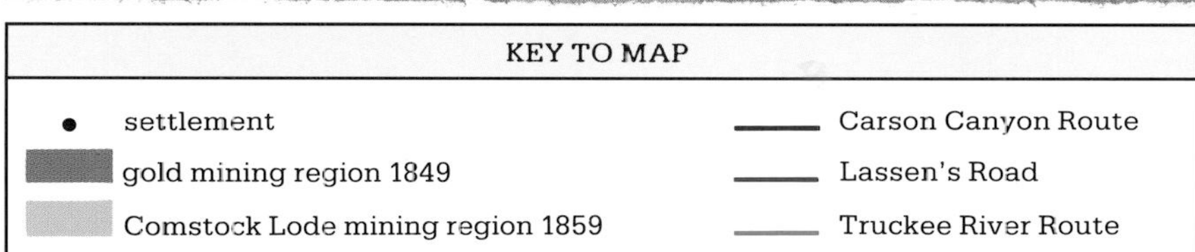

## REMEMBER THE ALAMO!

The valiant but tragic defense of the Alamo mission on March 6, 1836 has become one of American history's most oft-repeated legends – although historical research has revealed a few facts about the Alamo that often go unmentioned. For instance, Sam Houston, commander-in-chief of the Texas forces, never felt that the crumbling mission could stand up to a siege, and ordered frontiersman Jim Bowie (1796–1836) to destroy it in January. He didn't, however, and Provisional Governor Henry Smith promptly rescinded Houston's order and sent attorney-turned-colonel William B. Travis (?–1836) to defend it. The force that remained in the mission on February 23, the day the siege began, is estimated at between 182 and 188. Of these less than 20 were actually Texans; the rest, including Bowie and another frontier legend, Davy Crockett (1786–1836) were volunteers. Nearly all of them believed that reinforcements were only a short time away.

Thirteen days later, Santa Anna launched a pre-dawn attack. To the strains of the *Deguello* – a battle march indicating that "no quarter" would be given, or no prisoners taken – some 1,800 Mexican troops stormed the mission. They were thrown back by the rifles and cannon of the defenders; they rushed again, and were repulsed a second time. Eventually Santa Anna sent another wave of troops who broke the outer defenses and forced the Texans to retreat within the mission, fighting hand to hand.

**RIGHT** Celebrated Georgia-born frontiersman Jim Bowie – who reportedly designed the long-bladed Bowie knife, or "Arkansas Toothpick" – actually took part in the battle at the Alamo, though desperately ill at the time.

When the fighting was over, there were no survivors among the defenders. The myth that the garrison fought "to the last man", however, is not quite accurate, since evidence indicates that Davy Crockett and several others were captured and possibly tortured, then executed. That they died bravely has never been disputed. William Travis – who, at least according to legend, invited all who would stay and die with him to cross a line in the dirt – fell near a cannon at the north wall. And Jim Bowie, already deathly ill from a sickness that had recently claimed his wife and children, fought from his sickbed near the main gate. Like many others among the defenders, Bowie was armed with the formidable hunting-knife named for him.

The legendary defense of the Alamo served as a rallying point for the beleaguered Texans. Although Santa Anna, who lost at least 600 of some 3,000 troops against a force of less than 200, referred to the battle as "a small affair", the valor of the defenders gave the surviving Texan troops something to remember – and remember they did, six weeks later at San Jacinto.

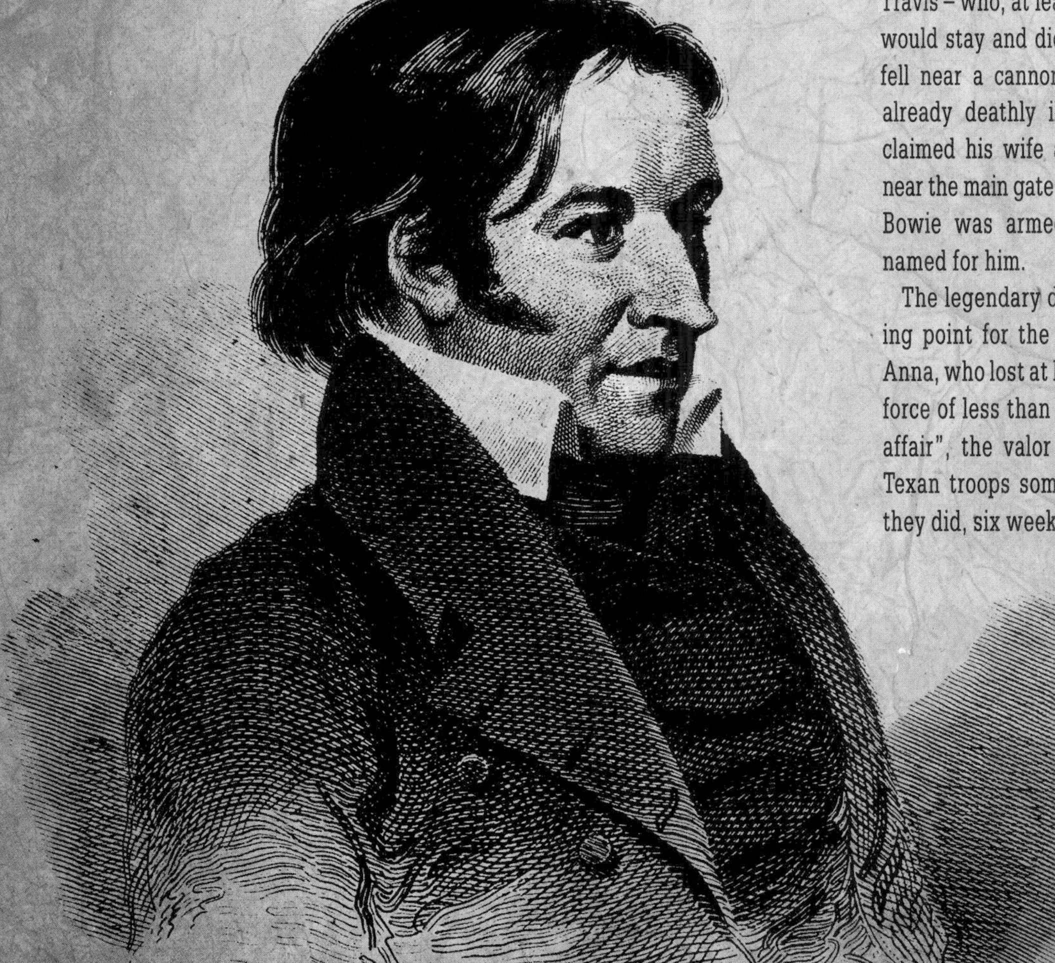

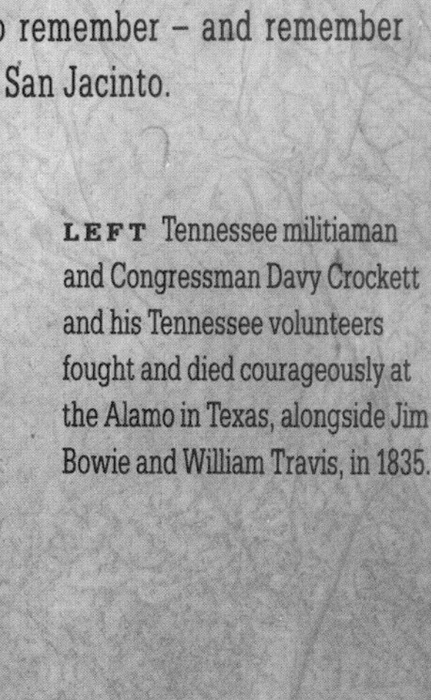

**LEFT** Tennessee militiaman and Congressman Davy Crockett and his Tennessee volunteers fought and died courageously at the Alamo in Texas, alongside Jim Bowie and William Travis, in 1835.

**ABOVE** When dawn rose on March 6, 1836 – the 13th and final day of the siege of the Alamo – General Santa Anna's Mexican troops charged the beleaguered mission, filling the air with the noise of battle and the sound of trumpets. A few hours later, all was quiet; every Texas defender was dead. But a new battle cry had been added to the annals of American history: "Remember the Alamo!"

**LEFT** As legend has it, Colonel Travis challenged the man of his command who were willing to fight to the last at the Alamo to step across a line he had drawn in the dirt. Only two men – Lewis Rose, who lived to escape and tell the story, and bedridden Jim Bowie – didn't cross the line, until Bowie convinced four fellow soldiers to carry him across.

# The 49ers

## The Discovery

It was found in the tailrace of a sawmill under construction on the American River in central California, on the morning of January 24, 1848. The property belonged to John Augustus Sutter (1803–80), a Swiss-born businessman who, with a grant from California's Mexican authorities, had built a 50,000-acre agricultural empire since arriving on the Pacific coast in 1839. The man who discovered it, James W. Marshall, was Sutter's carpenter in charge of the mill-building project some 40 miles away from Sutter's Fort, the company headquarters that for years had served as the destination of many emigrants traveling overland to California. It was to change the lives of thousands who would either discover or search in vain for it throughout California and other areas of the West. What was it? It was gold.

## The Rush

When Marshall confirmed his discovery and informed his employer that gold had indeed been found on his property, Sutter did the best he could to keep the news a secret. Although at heart a generous man, Sutter realized that his holdings – including farms, ranches and trading posts – could be jeopardized by the thousands of prospectors that would surely descend on his property if word of the discovery leaked.

John Sutter was, of course, absolutely right. Although it took several months to do so, the news of Marshall's discovery got out – and when it did Sutter's lands were overrun by goldseekers from everywhere, or so it seemed. They were part of perhaps the greatest short-term migration this or any other nation has ever seen: the California Gold Rush.

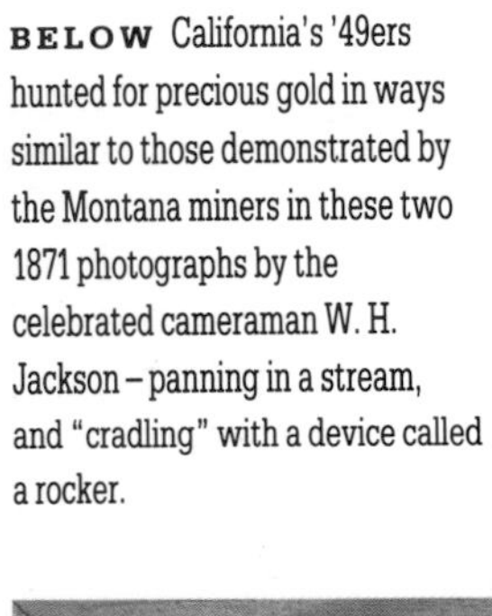

**BELOW** California's '49ers hunted for precious gold in ways similar to those demonstrated by the Montana miners in these two 1871 photographs by the celebrated cameraman W. H. Jackson – panning in a stream, and "cradling" with a device called a rocker.

**ABOVE** What started in California with the '49ers – the first miners and prospectors who rushed west in search of gold in 1849 – continued further east in the following two decades, when gold and silver strikes were made in the territories of Colorado, Nevada and Arizona. The strain of work shows in the faces of these San Miguel County, Colorado, miners.

The port of San Francisco, about 100 miles west of Sutter's Mill, was the first "city" (its population was around 800 at the time) to receive word of the gold strike. At first it fell on skeptical ears, but one man in particular – a Mormon merchant and publisher named Sam Brannan – took heed and started to think about the mercantile possibilities that the discovery of gold might present. After checking out the rumors by traveling to Sutter's Mill himself, Branna returned to San Francisco in May 1848 with a bottle of gold-dust in his hand and the word "gold" on his lips – shouted to anyone within earshot. The news traveled fast, and within weeks most of the men in the surrounding areas were off "prospecting". Sam Brannan was there too – but as a merchant, ready to supply the hordes of gold-seekers with the implements, foodstuffs and other goods they would need for their endeavors, at a handsome price.

By midsummer, it seemed as though all the men in California had disappeared into the hills. Soldiers and sailors left their posts, civilians dropped whatever they were doing to mine for gold. The first reports of the find had even reached the East – carried overland by none other than Kit Carson. Military men, including a young Lieutenant William Tecumseh Sherman, had surveyed the mines and re-

**RIGHT** To carry on their often fruitless and frustrating search for the mineral wealth of the West, prospectors required "grub" – and plenty of it, as evidenced by the number of spent food tins strewn about this typical Colorado mining camp of the 1860s.

**BELOW** Although they represented less than 10 per cent of the mining region's total population at the beginning of the gold rush, women later became fixtures in the towns, if not the camps, as shown in this 1884 photograph of male and female patrons in front of Hovey's Dance Hall in Clifton, Arizona.

ported to President Polk – who made the first official US Government pronouncement of the discovery in his annual address on December 5. From then on, it was, "California, here I come."

Gold fever had taken hold, and men from virtually everywhere set off for the goldfields, taking any conveyance or any route they could afford – by ship around Cape Horn or to and from Panama, overland by horse, wagon or on foot, following one of several established trails (the Mormon, Oregon or California). The "Argonauts" – or the 49ers, as they would later be called – were on their way.

## The Boom

The year 1849 would see the population of California Territory increase five-fold, from 20,000 to 100,000, due to the Gold Rush. In the mining area – roughly from the Sierra Nevada on the east to the line of the Feather, Sacramento and San Joaquin Rivers on the west, and from the Mariposa River in the south to the North Fork of the Feather in the north – mining camps and towns sprung up overnight. Their names pretty much told the story: Rough and Ready, You Bet, Fair Play, Hangtown, Liar's Flat, Volcano, Slumgullion and Growlersburg, to name only a few. Along with the miners, the camps were peopled with those who provided the goods and services the 49ers required – merchants, smiths, bartenders, preachers, gamblers and, of course, prostitutes.

**LEFT** Main Street, Creede, Colorado, on June 1, 1892. Four days later, the hastily constructed wooden buildings burned to the ground in a fire that swept the town.

**BELOW** From the onset of the Gold Rush in California in the late 1840s to the "closing" of the frontier four decades later, saloons like these were the salvation of many a thirsty, lonely prospector, cowboy or tracklayer in search of drink and companionship throughout the West.

**ABOVE** Where it all began: Sutter's original mill stood at this point on the South Fork of the American River in Coloma, California. It was here that James Marshall noticed, on the morning of January 24, 1848, the tiny yellow specks of gold that would change the fortunes of California – indeed, of the western US itself, forever.

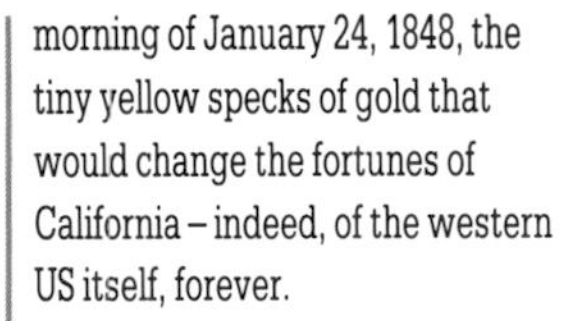

Gold from the mines brought unprecedented wealth into – and out of – the region. In one year alone (1852), California mines produced $81 million. Between 1848 and 1855, a staggering sum of $345 million worth of gold passed through San Francisco, which became a fully fledged city during the rush; its population boomed from 800 in 1848 to nearly 55,000 by 1855.

With all that money around, lawlessness was rampant in the brawling camps and towns. The bigger and busier the town, the more dangerous it became to walk the streets. In San Francisco, where the population soared, this was especially true. To

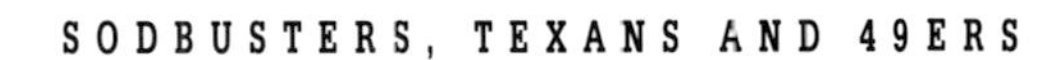

some, the only way to keep order was to form a "Committee of Vigilance" – the origin of the word "vigilante". San Francisco's first such committee was formed in 1851.

One celebrated incident involving the Committee of Vigilance focused on a crusading newspaper editor, James King (of William), who was apparently shot and killed by the target of his published criticism, corrupt politician James P. Casey, in May 1856. Casey's friends tried to protect him in jail, but the committee – and a small army organized for the occasion – seized Casey and another man, and hanged them both on May 22. So turned the wheels of justice during the chaos of the Gold Rush.

And justice, it seems, completely ignored the two men most connected with the Gold Rush – John Sutter and James Marshall. Sutter's vast empire was invaded, disrupted and nearly destroyed by hordes of prospectors, and he spent many years trying to get Government compensation for his loss. As for James Marshall, he never did strike gold himself; instead, he was so hounded by other prospectors trying to make his "luck" work for them that he was no longer welcome at most camps.

**LEFT** How it all began: A reconstruction of John Augustus Sutter's California sawmill, in which carpenter James W. Marshall found gold while testing the millrace.

**OPPOSITE, BOTTOM LEFT** One indispensable feature of the Western mining town . . . here, a citizen of Hazen, Nevada, stands outside the Shamrock Saloon in 1905.

**BELOW** In this 1895 photograph, an Oklahoma schoolmistress and her students pose stiffly in front of their typical prairie schoolhouse.

# RIVERMEN, RIDERS AND RAILROADERS

Although the earliest trail-blazers often traveled on foot or horseback, actually moving west as a pioneer meant finding a route and a "conveyance" for one's provisions, families and worldly possessions. Early on in the westward push, the continent's rivers, connected by canals, were the route, and the flatboat (and later the steamboat) the conveyance; soon trails or roads carved out of the wilderness carried horse-drawn wagons; eventually, the railroads covered the country and even connected East and West. Each of these methods of transport has contributed its share of legends to the story of the West.

## Wedding the Waters: DeWitt Clinton

The term "riverman" hardly applies to New York politician DeWitt Clinton (1769–1828), but he was instrumental in building the first great waterway to link the eastern US with what was then the most direct route to the interior of the continent – the Erie Canal, which effectively joined the Atlantic Ocean (via the Hudson River) to the Great Lakes. Opened in 1825, the great canal stretched across 363 miles from the Hudson at Albany to the Lake Erie port of Buffalo. It contained 83 locks which compensated for a 565-foot rise in elevation, and took nearly eight years to construct by blasting, hauling, digging and scraping earth away. A long-time mayor of New York City, Clinton led the effort to build the canal, at a total cost of $7 million.

The Erie Canal allowed passengers and freight to be carried on barges drawn by horses or mules on tracks alongside the waterway. The going was slow, but was considerably faster – and much cheaper – than overland routes; the canal cut travel time between New York and Buffalo by two weeks. The waterway was the crowning achievement of DeWitt Clinton's distinguished career. On November 4, 1825, it was he who poured a keg of Lake Erie water into New York – a "wedding of the waters" which officially opened the canal and inaugurated a new era in transportation between the East and the West.

**INSET** The Pony Express ran only between St Joseph, Missouri, and points west. Letters to and from points east went by US Postal Service. A Pony Express delivery took ten days.

# The Riders

Years after the rivermen had helped open the trans-Appalachian and "Old North-west" regions, including the Great Lakes area, to settlers, a new challenge presented itself to Americans – delivering mail to and from the newly opened lands west of the Rockies. In the 1850s, railroads and telegraph lines criss-crossed the East, so long-distance travel and communication were really not a problem there. But linking the Atlantic and Pacific coasts by rail was still years of tremendous labor away, nor did a transcontinental telegraph service yet exist – and with the effect of the recent Gold Rush inspiring new emigrants to flock to California, Oregon and other western territories in large quantities every day – other solutions were becoming desperately needed.

Among those solutions were two short-lived ventures that would none the less become a part of Western lore – the Butterfield Overland Mail Service and the Pony Express.

**BELOW** Ironically acknowledging the future of transcontinental communications as he swiftly delivers his mail, a Pony Express rider waves to workers erecting posts for the coast-to-coast telegraph line that, upon its completion in October 1861, will put the expressman out of a job.

AND PONY EXPRESS.—[PHOTOGRAPHED BY SAVAGE, SALT LAKE CITY, FROM A PAINTING BY GEORGE M. OTTINGER.]

**RIGHT** The US Rail network proved to be of vital significance during the Civil War – which was why it was destroyed on such a grand scale. These tracks near Atlanta show a sample of the devastation that was to follow.

## The Butterfield Overland Mail Service

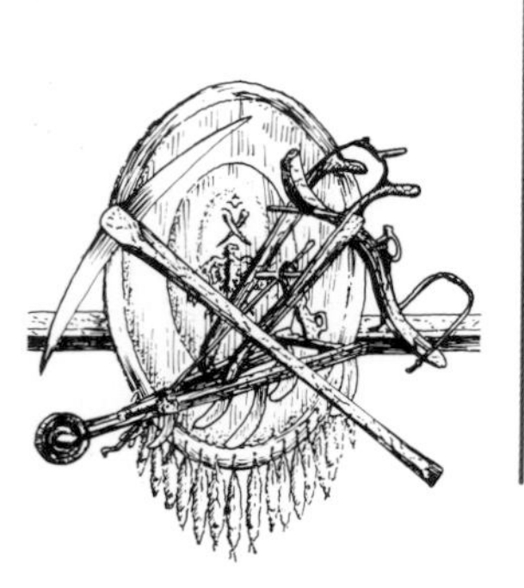

Begun by entrepreneur John Butterfield in 1858, the Butterfield line stretched some 2,800 miles from Tipton, Missouri (west of St Louis) to San Francisco, in an "ox-bow" pattern that skirted the border between the south-western territories and Mexico. The line carried passengers and mail in "celerity wagons" – light covered vehicles that were high in speed but low in comfort. These coaches progressed in stages (hence the name "stagecoach"), night and day, along a route connected by 165 stations where men and horses were changed.

The entire run took about 24 days – meaning that the skilled Butterfield drivers took their wagons across rugged country at a breakneck pace for the time, averaging 120 miles per day, and often fighting off attacks by bandits and hostile Indians. The service came to an end in 1861, when a transcontinental telegraph line, promoted in part by Butterfield himself, was completed.

**LEFT** Beginning in 1858, the innovative Butterfield Overland Mail Service carried the US Mail and passengers by stagecoach between Missouri and San Francisco along the southern border of the US in 24 days. When the transcontinental telegraph shut the BOMS down in 1861, its president John Butterfield (1801–69) sold the line to Wells Fargo, with whom he had been partners in yet another venture – American Express.

**BELOW** Larger and heavier than the swift "celerity wagons" used by the Butterfield Overland Mail Service – the West's first true "stage coach" line – this Concord stagecoach, photographed in 1869, was typical of the coaches that carried passengers and shipments throughout the West from the 1850s.

**RIGHT** The legendary riders of the Pony Express achieved the "swift completion of their appointed rounds" by traveling extremely light, often armed with only knife and pistol, and changing horses (every 15 miles) in about two minutes.

**BELOW** Pony Express partner Alexander Majors (seen here) was in the end proved right about the inherent unprofitability of the freighting firm – the company lost $200,000 on the deal.

## The Pony Express

Better known – but even shorter-lived – than the Butterfield line was the fabled Pony Express, a system that sent lone riders galloping across 1,966 miles of plains, mountains and deserts to deliver the US mail from St Joseph, Missouri to Sacramento, California (formerly the site of Sutter's Fort). The brainchild of William H. Russell, a partner in the freighting firm of Russell, Majors & Waddell, the Pony Express began operations for the US Government in April 1860.

The Pony Express line consisted of 25 "home stations" where riders were changed (approximately every 75 miles), and 165 "swing stations" where riders changed horses about every 15 miles. The nearly 2,000 mile run took about 10 days to complete, and followed the Platte River, across the Rockies through South Pass, over the Utah desert and through the Sierras to Sacramento – some of

the most dangerous and punishing territory in the continent. The Pony Express riders were young (about 19 years old on average), small and tough. William ("Buffalo Bill") Cody was one of them. Aged only 15 at the time, Cody once arrived at a relay station to find his relief dead, so he completed the next run, and returned – logging a total of 322 miles in one trip.

The extraordinary accomplishments of the Pony Express – carrying nearly 35,000 pieces of mail over some 650,000 miles in only 18 months – ended in October 1861, a casualty of the coast-to-coast telegraph line. Ironically, Russell and his partners lost almost $200,000 on the enterprise, and received nothing from the Government – but the Pony Express left a legendary reputation as a venture representing "Yankee ingenuity" at its finest.

**ABOVE** Frank Webner, a Pony Express rider, in 1861. In the 19 months the Pony Express existed, only one rider was killed by hostile Indians, and only one bag of mail was lost. The riders had covered 650,000 miles on horseback.

## THE BRAWLING BOATMAN: MIKE FINK

The men who navigated America's rivers and canals in the first half of the 19th century were a hardy and colorful lot – similar in many ways (including temperament) to the tough mountain men and scouts who penetrated the wilderness, and about as far from cultured men like DeWitt Clinton as one could get. From the scrappy "canawlers" who guided mule-drawn barges full of emigrants or goods down the canals, to the flatboatmen and keelboatmen who propelled their craft upriver with oars or poles, the rivermen were a brawling breed. One such legendary character was Mike Fink (*c.* 1770–?), a Pittsburgh-born keelboatman who described himself as "half horse and half alligator". Fink, who began his colorful career before 1800 as an oarsman on keelboats running up and down the Mississippi and Ohio Rivers, used his considerable riverman's skills – as well as his fists – to battle his way to the captaincy of his own boat.

According to the yarn-spinners of the western rivers, Mike Fink never lost one of the knock-down, drag'em-out fist fights that were the rivermen's trademark. And his marksmanship was also legendary; a contemporary engraving depicts him shooting a cup of whiskey off the head of a trusting friend, who presumably survived the stunt. Although Fink exchanged the riverman's life for that of a fur trapper in the 1820s, when the success of the Robert Fulton's steamboat marked the beginning of the end for the keelboats, his exact fate is not known; it is likely that he was shot by the friend of a trapper he killed during another display of marksmanship at a winter camp in the Rockies.

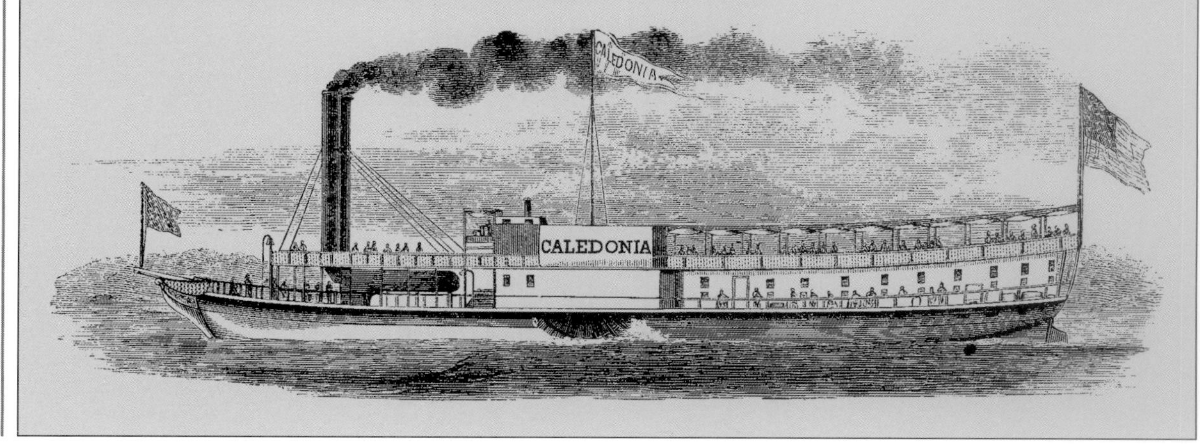


**RIGHT** Some brawling rivermen, like the semi-legendary Mike Fink, literally took to the hills as trappers when steamboats such as the one in this engraving – *The Caledonia, c.* 1819 – gradually replaced flatboats on the busy Mississippi and Ohio Rivers in the 1820s.

**LEFT** Along with that of his shy partner Henry Wells, the name of dynamic express entrepreneur William G. Fargo (1810–81) has been immortalized in song, story and the still-thriving security and express business they formed during the California Gold Rush – Wells, Fargo & Company; Fargo is also honored by North Dakota's largest city.

## THE WELLS-FARGO WAGON

Perhaps the most impressive record of transporting goods and mail throughout the West – especially freight of high value – belongs to a legendary firm that still exists today: Wells, Fargo and Company. Founded in San Francisco in 1852 and controlled by Henry Wells and William G. Fargo from the East, the firm originally shipped gold from the Pacific coast by sea, but eventually included overland stagecoach service for mail, goods and valuables. The company contracted with local stage and ship lines to carry the goods, and provided nearly every kind of shipping service. By the time of the Civil War – after it had bought out part of the defunct Butterfield Overland operations, Wells–Fargo was synonymous with "express" throughout the West, from the Missouri to the Pacific, and it was the only overland link between East and West. To thousands of emigrants on the Western frontier, the approach of the "Wells–Fargo wagon" meant that a long-awaited shipment of goods or mail had arrived. After the transcontinental railroad was completed in 1869, Wells, Fargo & Company focused on providing service between rail lines; the company survived the "closing" of the West, and continued into the next century by providing a service that has since become yet another image of American culture – the "armored car", carrying payroll shipments and other highly valued cargoes to their destinations throughout the US.

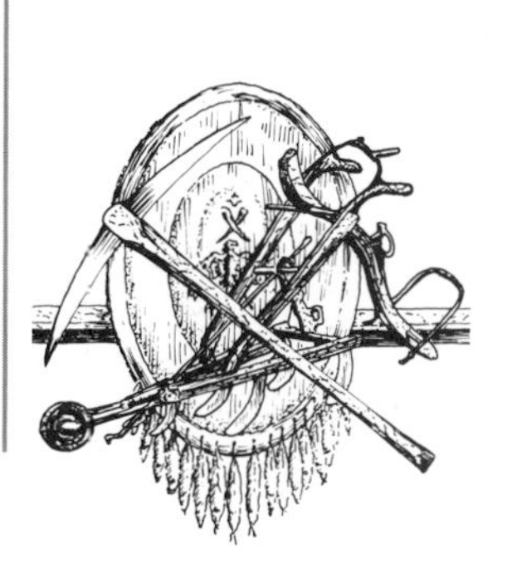

# Working on the Railroad

Undoubtedly, the coming of the railroads changed the face of the American nation, both East and West. Since the trial run of America's first steam locomotive in 1830, railroads had slowly brought communities and regions closer together as more miles of track were laid and more lines began operations on both coasts. As the great migration to the West began in earnest in the 1840s, the idea of a transcontinental railroad began to command attention. Such visionaries as New York merchant Asa Whitney proposed that companies be given land grants on which they would not only lay tracks across the continent but also promote settlement by selling land to emigrants. Toward the end of that decade, surveyors and explorers – including John C. Frémont on an ill-fated 1848 expedition – began searching out routes for the great undertaking.

After enduring years of talk about a transcontinental railroad, a young railroad engineer named Theodore Dehone Judah (1826–63) published, in 1857, "A Practical Plan for Building the Pacific Railroad". Improving his plan over the next several years, Judah

**OPPOSITE, FAR RIGHT** History about to happen: Hundreds of onlookers crowd the tracks at Promontory, Utah, on May 10, 1869, as crews and dignitaries from the Central Pacific and Union Pacific Railroads prepare to complete the Transcontinental Railroad track by driving in a final spike, fashioned from 18 oz. of gold. Incidentally, both Leland Stanford of the CP and Thomas Durant of the UP swung – and missed.

**RIGHT** History relived: At Golden Spike National Historical Site in Promontory, Utah, replicas of two legendary steam locomotives, the Central Pacific's *Jupiter* and the Union Pacific's *No. 119,* touch cowcatchers, recreating the moment in 1869 that symbolized the linking of America's coasts – the completion of the Transcontinental Railroad.

procured the financial backing of several Sacramento, California, businessmen, four of whom – California Governor Leland Stanford (1824–?), Charles Crocker (1822–?), Mark Hopkins (1813–78) and Collis P. Huntington (1821–1900), later known as the "Big Four" – formed the Central Pacific Railroad in 1861, with Judah as their Chief Engineer. The CP, as it became known, received authorization from the US Government to build part of the transcontinental railroad, eastward from Sacramento, crossing the Sierras – as Judah had suggested – at the fabled Donner Pass.

Although ground was broken for the project on January 8, 1863 in Sacramento, money manipulations by the Big Four angered Judah; before they could be straightened out the engineer died of yellow fever which he had contracted in Panama years before. Charles Crocker took direct control of construction, and work on the CP tracks continued, although the Civil War and labor problems slowed things down considerably.

At the same time, the Union Pacific Railroad was formed to build the eastern portion of the line, starting in Nebraska. The UP's president, Thomas Durant, was in fact a schemer who earned millions through shady dealings during the building of the railroad. He was never convicted of wrong-doing, although many of his associates were ruined. As for the railroad itself, no real construction began until after the Civil War had ended.

Between 1865 and 1869, crews from both the CP and the UP pulled off a construction miracle. Chinese coolies hired by Charles Crocker laid the Central Pacific tracks from Sacramento, while UP crews comprised mostly of Irish immigrants and Civil War veterans built the eastern leg of the railroad. The UP crews were spurred on by brothers Jack and Dan Casement who inspired their men to lay track at a frenetic pace, earning Jack the title of "Champion Tracklayer of the Continent".

The crews of both railroads worked without bulldozers, steam-shovels or any other "heavy equipment". They used picks, shovels, dump carts and hammers. In the end, after five years of brutal work in rugged country – which was still vulnerable to Indian attack – the combined UP and CP crews laid a total of 1,776 miles of track across the United States. Although the two crews were actually in competition with each other – the first to complete its part would collect Government grants and bonds – they finally met at an agreed-upon spot: Promontory, Utah, just north of the Great Salt Lake. On May 10, 1869, the final spike – made of gold – was driven in by Leland Stanford, and the nation rejoiced; finally there was a railroad to link the East Coast of the US with the West.

**ABOVE** Tent camps such as this one near Nevada's Humboldt River Canyon were home to the thousands of Chinese workers who carved the Central Pacific Railroad's portion of the Transcontinental line through the Western mountains – visible behind the construction train in this 1868 photograph.

**LEFT** Charged with overseeing the entire Union Pacific tracklaying operation for the Transcontinental Railroad with his brother Dan, Jack Casement – photographed along the line, whip in hand, in 1869 – drove his predominantly Irish crews sternly but fairly. Keeping his men in line, fighting off Indians and controlling hangers-on, Casement got the job done, and earned the title of "Champion Tracklayer of the Continent".

# WESTERN WOMEN

**RIGHT** The early leaders of the suffrage movement in the US were usually also advocates of temperance and of the abolition of slavery. After the Fifteenth Amendment (1870) gave the franchise to newly emancipated black men, but not to the women who had helped them win it, the suffragists mostly confined their efforts to the struggle for the vote. Wyoming was the first state to extend democracy to women, as witnessed by this 1870 picture of Mrs D. S. Sonneburger, casting the first vote for women in Johnson County.

lthough history – the majority of which has been written by men – may have often overlooked them, a great many women have earned their own places in the history of the American West. In roles ranging from gunfighters, prostitutes and gamblers to surveyors, missionaries and wilderness guides, these women helped to shape the West as much as their male counterparts did. In fact, some did even more.

## Sacajawea Saves the Corps of Discovery

One particularly interesting example of a woman's contribution to the building of the West is chronologically the first one – and also probably the most important from a historical standpoint. After all, if the Lewis and Clark Expedition of 1804–6 had not accomplished all it did, the history of the United States' westward expansion might have turned out very differently. One woman – the Shoshoni Sacajawea – deserves a great deal of credit for the success and survival of the Corps of Discovery.

Both Lewis and Clark credit Sacajawea, the teenaged wife of the apparently loathsome French-Canadian trapper Toussaint Charbonneau, with saving the Corps of Discovery from interference – if not outright attack – by other Native American tribes, more than once. She served as an interpreter and guide, and her presence often seemed to convince otherwise skeptical Indians of the corps' peaceful intentions. Born a Shoshoni, but captured by another tribe as a child, Sacajewea encountered her long-lost brother, a Shoshoni chief, and thereby secured help – and horses – for the expedition. Remarkably, Sacajawea was about 16 years old and some months pregnant when she joined the expedition; she gave birth to a son, Baptiste (given the nickname "Pomp" by the captains), along the trail.

Sacajawea's ultimate legacy was the great geographic, scientific and cultural knowledge gathered by the Corps of Discovery.

# "My most happy life-work": Jessie Benton Frémont

**LEFT** When Jessie Benton, daughter of Missouri Senator Thomas Hart Benton, outraged her father by secretly marrying future explorer John Charles Frémont, she stood firmly by her ambitious husband, declaring, "Wither thou goest, I will go." Jessie did just that, and her writing talent was responsible in large part for the dazzling reports of John's expeditions that fired the public's interest in the West.

Some 40 years later, a woman propelled the knowledge gathered by another western expedition into a document that captured the imagination of the people and the Government of the United States. She was Jessie Benton Frémont, the beautiful, gifted daughter of Senator Thomas Hart Benton and wife of Army explorer John Charles Frémont.

Upon her husband's return from his first expedition to the Rockies in late 1842, Jessie – who had just given birth to her first daughter – wrote a 207-page report of the expedition from John's dictation and, in her words, "thus slid into my most happy life-work." She was indeed talented; the report, which was presented to Congress in March 1843 and subsequently published, stirred the American public's interest in the Great West, and thoroughly promoted the cause of "Manifest Destiny". It also helped John secure the backing for more expeditions. Ironically, when the Frémont fortunes began to wane some 30 years later, it was Jessie's writing talent that supported John and their children.

# Of Stars and Spies

Talent of another kind figures in a few colorful legends concerning women who originally ventured West as performers.

## Lovely Lola Montez

Born Marie Gilbert in Ireland, Lola Montez (1818–61) began a career as a "Spanish dancer" in London in 1843. She appeared throughout Europe in the '40s, and a series of well-publicized marriages and liaisons – including one with the King of Bavaria – brought the dazzling beauty a notoriety that followed her to New York in 1851, then to New Orleans and finally to San Francisco in the autumn of 1853.

At the height of the Gold Rush, Lola performed throughout the mining region, gaining a reputation for a quick temper and handiness with a whip when confronting critics. She also married again, invested in

**FAR RIGHT** The short life of 19th-century stage star Adah Isaacs Menken – who died as a result of an onstage accident at 33 – saw the New Orleans-born actress become famous, as much for her romantic exploits as for her acting, in London, Paris, New York and the American West. Menken's legendary appearances in *Mezeppa,* bound to a horse and in simulated nudity, electrified audiences from Vienna to Virginia City.

**RIGHT** Dancing her way from Ireland to the California mining region via the capitals of Europe, Marie Gilbert – better known as Lola Montez – made headlines with a hot temper and even hotter romantic relationships. Never a great dancer, Montez often silenced critics with her ever-ready whip, and her offstage exploits delighted the citizens of the mining towns.

mining concerns and bought a home in Grass Valley, retiring from the stage in 1856 to write a series of beauty manuals. Returning seriously ill to New York from a British lecture tour in the late 1850s, Lola Montez took up religion, visited other ill women at local asylums, and died in a Brooklyn boarding-house at the age of 43. Her Grass Valley cottage stands today as a memorial.

## A Daring Dancer: Adah Isaacs Menken

An actress and poet renowned on two continents, Adah Isaacs Menken (*c.* 1835–68) made a ballet début as a child in her native New Orleans, then performed in Cuba and Texas. Highly educated, she studied poetry, the Romance languages, German, Hebrew, voice, dance and riding. Thus prepared, she launched her adult theatrical career in New Orleans in 1857, having wed Alexander Isaac Menken the year before – the first of four short-lived marriages (upon her divorce, Adah kept Menken's middle and last names, but added an "s" to Isaac). She began a successful New York stage career (and married her second husband, a prize-fighter) in 1859; she first performed her most famous role in *Mazeppa (or the Wild Horse of Tartary)* in an Albany theatre in 1861.

In the title role of the hapless heroine of this melodrama based on Byron's poem, Adah appeared on stage, apparently nude (although actually in a body stocking) and bound to what one can only hope was a well-trained horse. As one can imagine, this scene electrified audiences wherever she played it – and in 1863, she played it in San Francisco, Salt Lake City and Virginia City, where the miners were so thrilled that they made Adah an honorary fireman. She continued her theatrical success in Britain and Europe, where she also wrote poetry and befriended the likes of Dickens, Dumas, Swinburne, Rossetti and George Sand. Adah Isaacs Menken's life on stage and off always made good copy, and she was loved throughout the West; tragically, she died in Paris at the age of 33 from complications of an earlier injury sustained while playing Mazeppa.

# A GALLERY OF WESTERN "WILDCATS"

Not all of these legendary ladies of the West were "bad", but they certainly left historians something to talk about.

### GERTRUDIS BARCELO: "DONA TULES" (?–1852)

This legendary New Mexico gambler became an expert monte dealer and eventually ran an opulent *sala* in Santa Fe. At her peak, the beautiful, cigar-smoking "Dona Tules" made a fortune; in declining years she grew very rich and very fat.

### JULIA BULETTE (?–1867)

One of the Nevada mining region's most beloved prostitutes, London-born Julia came to the States with her family, taking to the streets in California and in Virginia City in the early 1860s. Friendly and attractive, she was a volunteer firewoman as well as a whore; Virginia City was shocked when she was murdered in a robbery at her home in 1867.

### MARTHA JANE CANARY: "CALAMITY JANE" (*c.*1848–1903)

Not an outlaw, but a good shot who drank, drifted, brawled and cussed her way through the West from the mid-60s on. Often disguised as a man, she tramped along with the Union Pacific as it was built, served as an Army teamster, and rendered distinguished service as a nurse during an 1870s smallpox epidemic in Dakota. Dying poor in Deadwood, "Calamity Jane" was buried next to Wild Bill Hickok.

### PEARL HART

Pearl, not the brightest of outlaws, was a mining-camp cook in Arizona when she agreed to help a drunken miner, Joe Boot, attempt what turned out to be the last stagecoach robbery in the West. They were caught by a posse after getting lost. Joe got 35 years; Pearl got five, was released after two and a half, and faded into obscurity in Kansas City.

**RIGHT** Martha "Calamity Jane" Canary roared through an unsteady but ultimately legendary career as a hard-drinking muleskinner, teamster, scout, nurse, Wild West Show performer and occasional prostitute.

**RIGHT** Belle Starr, as portrayed in an 1886 issue of the *National Police Gazette*. In 1883, she was the first woman to be tried and convicted for a major crime – horse theft.

### ANNIE MCDOULET AND JENNIE STEVENS: "CATTLE ANNIE AND LITTLE BRITCHES"

These two teens, known as "Oklahoma's Girl Bandits", were really no more than juvenile delinquents who hooked up with the Doolin–Dalton gang. In 1394, Bill Tilghman and his deputy caught up with them, spanked them and sent them to jail. Released after two years, they then went straight.

### ANNIE OAKLEY (1860–?)

Annie was definitely not an outlaw, but a legendary performer with a rifle. She began shooting game around the age of nine; by 15 she could outshoot most men, including exhibition-shooter Frank Butler, her future husband. Annie began wowing audiences with her marksmanship all over the country in Buffalo Bill Cody's Wild West Show in 1885, and continued to do so for the next 17 years.

### ETTA PLACE

Fabled as the lover of Harry Longbaugh ("The Sundance Kid"), it is very likely that Etta did take part in robberies with the Kid and Butch Cassidy, notably the hold up of UP Train No. 03 in August 1900, dressed as a man. She did not, however, die in the Argentina ambush that killed Butch and Sundance, since she was undergoing surgery on her appendix at the time.

### FLO QUICK: "TOM KING"

The mistress of famed outlaw Bob Dalton, "Tom" rustled cattle in the Indian Territory in the 1880s, wheedled information out of train men for the Daltons and even led a gang of train robbers herself in the early '90s; rumor has it she was shot in a hold up – dressed, as always, in men's clothes.

### BELLE STARR (1848–89)

Born Myra Belle Shirley and well educated but "wild" in youth, she became one of the West's most infamous women. Possibly a teenaged Confederate courier during the Civil War, Belle later planned robberies throughout the West, stole horses, bribed officials, sheltered fugitives and shared the bed of many an outlaw – including Cole Younger, who she claimed was the father of her daughter Pearl – and married outlaw Sam Starr. The "Bandit Queen" was murdered in 1889 – shotgunned in the back – by persons unknown.

**LEFT** Petite Annie Oakley (1860–1926) was a sharpshooting star with Buffalo Bill's Wild West Show for nearly two decades.

**LEFT** Annie McDougal (Cattle Annie, left) and Jennie Metcalf (Little Britches, right) were allegedly involved in just about every illegal activity the era had to offer, including peddling whiskey to Indians, rustling horses and cattle, highway robbery and bank robbery. When they were finally apprehended they were sent back East to reform school.

## Union Spy: "Major Pauline Cushman"

A contemporary of Adah Menken's, Pauline Cushman (1835–93) was also an actress born in New Orleans in 1835, but her ultimately tragic life took quite a different turn. Pauline grew up on the Michigan frontier, ventured to New York at 18, and was hired there for an engagement in New Orleans which began a bright career. But while touring in Louisville at the beginning of the Civil War, an on-stage "toast" to the Confederacy started Pauline on a brief career as a Union spy, smuggling messages out of the South, sometimes baked into bread. Eventually caught, she was sentenced to hang as a spy, but was spared by a Rebel retreat.

After her rescue, Pauline conducted a lecture tour about her adventures – dressed in a Union uniform and billed as Major Pauline Cushman – then married and settled down in Michigan. Within a few years she had seven children. But by 1871, she had lost them all – four to diphtheria on the same day, and the others later, along with her husband. Picking up the pieces of her life, Pauline headed west to San Francisco and began a strange new existence, running various profitable businesses throughout California and Arizona – hotels, hunting lodges, roadhouses – and acquiring a Lola Montez-like reputation for toughness and a quick whip-hand. But years later Pauline died at the age of 58 in relative poverty in San Francisco.

## The "Measuring Woman": Alice Fletcher

It was this same quest for peace and understanding between Indians and white men that inspired the work of Alice Fletcher (1838–1923), known to several Native American tribes as the "Measuring Woman". At the age of 43, Alice travelled to Nebraska in 1881 to live among the Omaha, Ponca, Winnebago and Nez Perce tribes and learn their ways. Becoming an Indian agent in 1883, she directed the job of surveying land allotments to these tribes, which took nearly two years. Her fieldwork earned her a fellowship at the Peabody Museum at Harvard, which she held for a quarter of a century.

## Queen of the Cowgirls: Ann Willis

Although the Western frontier was rapidly closing during her childhood, Ann Bassett Willis (1878–1956) was a cowgirl from the start. Born on her father's small ranch in Brown's Hole, Colorado, during a raging snowstorm, she was nursed by an Indian neighbor for her first six months. She grew up in "God's country", the beautiful Green River valley, and learned to rope the cattle and ride the Arabian horses raised on the Bassett family's ranch. Always spunky, pretty, teenaged Ann raised a little hell on horseback in the Boston finishing-school she attended, and charmed the young men back home in Brown's Park – including local boy Butch Cassidy.

In 1900, at 22, she testified against hired gunman Tom Horn, convinced that he had shot a childhood friend. But it was as a small rancher who wouldn't hesitate to criticize the large cattle companies that Ann Bassett made her mark. She was continually outspoken about large herds that were allowed to trample the grazing lands of small ranches – and eventually, in 1911–12, found herself charged with rustling. Ann maintained her innocence throughout, and the charges were later found to have been trumped up. "Queen Ann", as she was often called, later married Frank Willis and ranched in California and Utah. She lived to the ripe old age of 78 – spunky to the last.

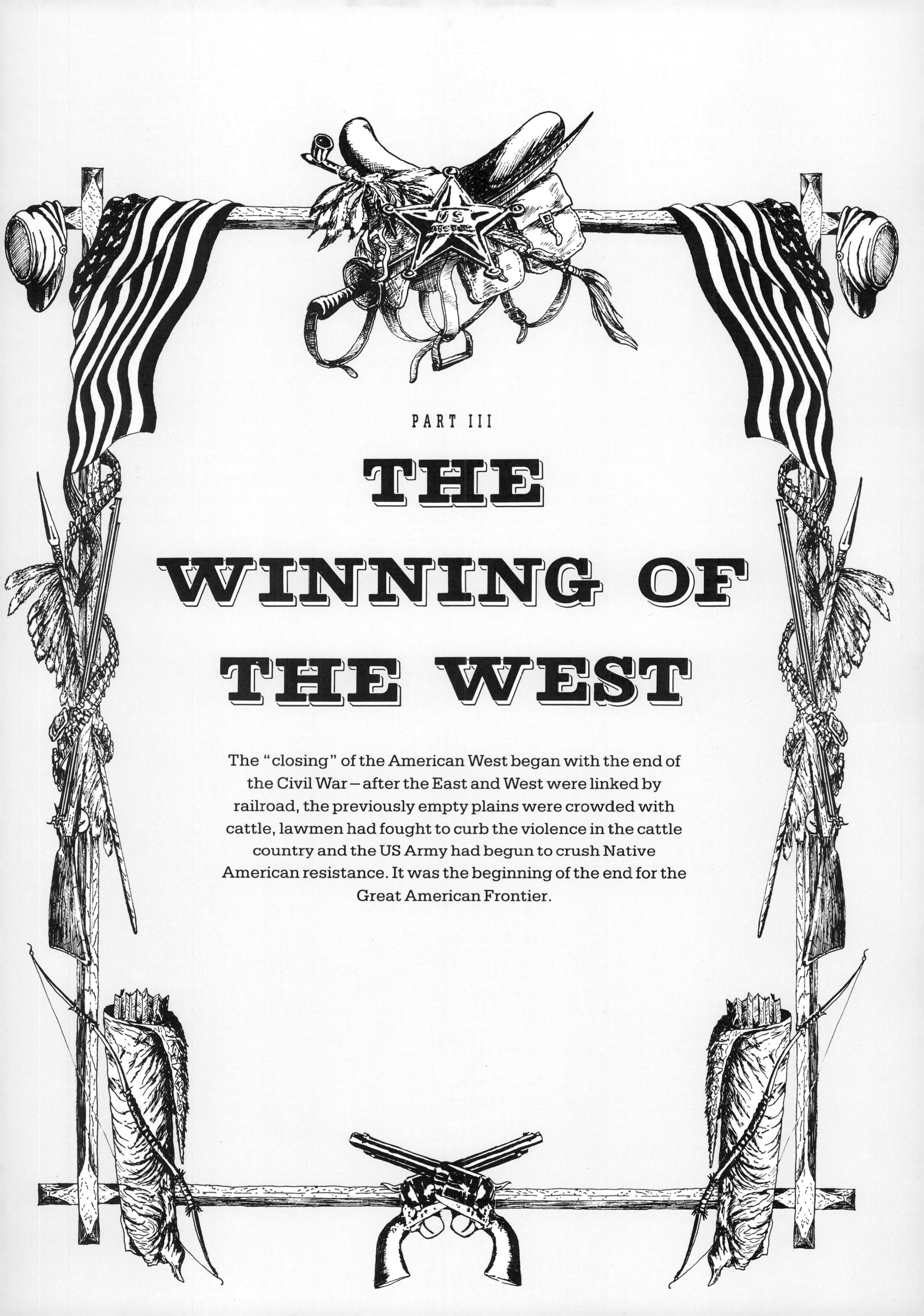

PART III

# THE WINNING OF THE WEST

The "closing" of the American West began with the end of the Civil War – after the East and West were linked by railroad, the previously empty plains were crowded with cattle, lawmen had fought to curb the violence in the cattle country and the US Army had begun to crush Native American resistance. It was the beginning of the end for the Great American Frontier.

# COWBOYS, GUNSLINGERS AND LAWMEN

**BELOW** Tombstone, Arizona, was among the typically "wicked" towns that sprung up throughout the West when cattle was king. In reality, like many other legendarily "bloody" cowtowns, Tombstone averaged only about four or five homocides per year.

The 1860s and '70s saw the rise of the cowboys and cattle barons in the Western plains – and as cow towns sprung up, they often housed their share of rustlers, robbers and hired guns – along with a "peace officer" paid to keep the unsavory elements in check. Although today legendary for their mythic violence, "bad" towns like Abilene, Deadwood, Tombstone and Dodge City really only saw a few killings each year – but those who did the killing, and some of their victims, became part of the great legends of the West.

# The Cowboys Move In

Texas cattle had been around for hundreds of years, but no one paid much attention to the herds until the 1850s and '60s, when what Texas had been lacking – a market for the cattle – emerged in new Missouri rail lines, which could then ship the cows to the eastern markets. Just as the Civil War ended, the day of the cattlemen began.

The first "Long Drive" of Texas cattle northward to the Missouri rail heads in 1866 was a fiasco, plagued by bad weather, stampedes, attacks by former Confederate guerillas and the resistance of Missouri farmers afraid of "Texas Fever" infecting their animals. The herds were backed up, and many cattle died of starvation. The drive had been a bust – and would always be so unless new trails to new markets were blazed.

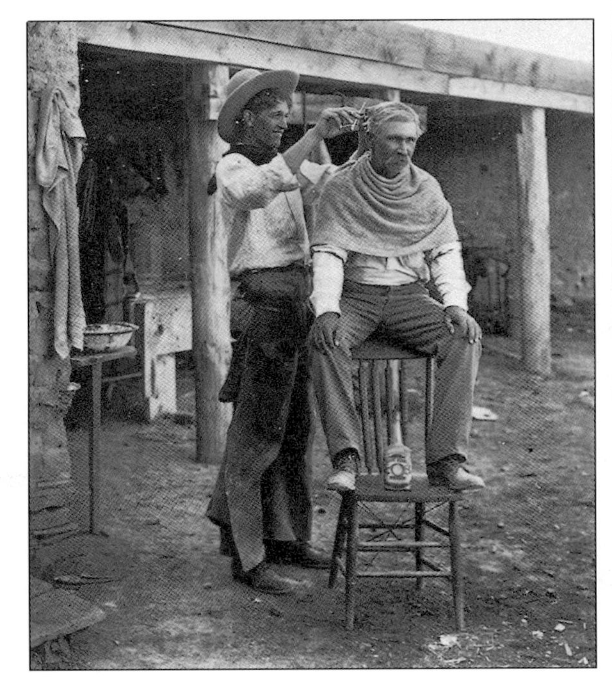

**ABOVE** The roundup, prior to the long drive north, represented the heart and soul of the American cattle business. This scene was played out many thousands of times by cowboys throughout the vast "cow country" of the western plains.

**LEFT** Of necessity, cowboys were self-sufficient sorts. Some developed rough-and-ready skills in doctoring – cows, horses and men – while others provided that essential service, haircuts.

## A GALLERY OF BADMEN

### CLAY ALLISON (1840-87)

Clay was a Confederate veteran from Tennessee who fought his way up from foreman to ranch owner in New Mexico, then worked as a hired gun for cattlemen enforcing their range rights. He earned a reputation as a vicious killer, especially when drunk; he was under the influence when he fell from his wagon and broke his neck under a wheel in 1887.

### SAM BASS (1851-78)

This illiterate Indiana native drifted to and from Texas, Kansas, the Dakotas and Nebraska – gambling and robbing trains along the way, until a friend betrayed him and he was killed by lawmen at Round Rock, aged 27.

### BILLY THE KID (1859-81)

The infamous Kid, whose name may have been Bonney, was an Army teamster at 18 when he killed a blacksmith; jailed, he escaped and wound up as a hired gun in New Mexico's Lincoln County War, in which he shot a sheriff. Billy claimed to have shot 21 men, but four may be closer to the truth; he was about to hang when he escaped, but the Kid was tracked down and shot by lawman Pat Garrett.

### BUTCH CASSIDY AND THE SUNDANCE KID

Born Robert Parker and Harry Longbaugh, this notorious pair became cattle rustlers in the mid-90s, gaining fame as leaders of the "Wild Bunch". They moved into train robberies later, and disappeared in South America after the turn of the century – possibly dying in a shoot-out in 1909 near La Paz.

**ABOVE** Much about Billy the Kid is unknown, including his real name (historians argue whether it was Henry McCarty or William H. Bonney) and his date of birth. This picture of Billy holding a carbine was taken around 1879.

**LEFT** The Wild Bunch. From left to right: Harry Longbaugh ("The Sundance Kid"), William Carver, Ben Kilpatrick, Harvey Logan and Robert Parker ("Butch Cassidy").

### THE DALTON GANG

Brothers Emmett, Bob and Gratton Dalton were lawmen for a time, but followed the lead of the James–Younger Gang and turned train robbers in 1890 with Bill Doolin. In October 1892, the gang was recognized after a hold up and blasted by citizens inside one of the banks; of the brothers, only Emmett survived.

### JOHN WESLEY HARDIN (1853–95)

One of the West's most vicious killers, Hardin was a racist who often dispatched men simply for their color. He claimed to have killed 41 men, and was probably telling the truth. Ironically, his gun jammed when caught by Texas Rangers; taken alive, he spent only 15 years in prison and came out a lawyer, but was shot in the back by a disgruntled lawman.

**LEFT** Unlike Billy the Kid, John Wesley Hardin didn't lie about the number of his victims, of which at least 41 are known. Incredibly, this Wild West version of a racist serial killer was never hanged for his crimes, but was shot in the back on release from a 15-year prison sentence.

**BELOW** On October 5, 1892, the citizens of Coveyville, Kansas, were lying in wait for the Dalton Gang as they tried to rob the town's two banks. Four gang members were shot in the ensuing gun battle. From left to right: Bill Powers, Bob Dalton, Grat Dalton and Dick Broadwell.

## The New Trails

**RIGHT** Wyoming's Laramie Plain was the northernmost destination of cattle driven along the Goodnight–Loving trail, later extended from an original trail blazed from Texas to New Mexico by partners Charles Goodnight (pictured here) and Oliver Loving in 1866.

The trail to the Wyoming range was blazed by ranching partners Charles Goodnight and Oliver Loving, who drove their first herd over it in 1866. The Goodnight–Loving Trail led west from central Texas into New Mexico, then north through Colorado and on to Wyoming's Laramie Plain. There, a few years earlier in the spring of 1865, a cowboy named E. S. Newman discovered that his cattle had survived the winter by digging through the snow to the grassland underneath – thus proving that the vast northern plains were suitable for ranching. Trails like Chisholm's and Goodnight's blazed the way to these northern ranges, where over the next three decades the cattlemen would reign supreme.

Among the first new trails the Texas cattlemen followed north in the late 1860s were wagon tracks left by a half-Cherokee trader named Jesse Chisholm (*c.* 1806–68), who journeyed from his post in Kansas to trade with tribes in the Indian Territory. Highly respected by whites and Indians alike for his honesty and kindness, Chisholm never drove cattle; but his tracks were followed by cowboys driving herds north to Kansas – and the cattle trail that later developed bore his name.

**RIGHT** The earliest cattlemen to lead their herds north from Texas in the 1860s followed a trail worn by the tracks of Jesse Chisolm's wagons as they traveled to railheads in the vicinity of Abilene, Kansas. Chisolm, a half-Cherokee Tennessean who reportedly spoke 14 Native American dialects, was a respected trader who had operated first near Fort Smith, Arkansas, and later on the Texas–Kansas route.

## The Johnson County War

Since coming into their own in the 1860s and '70s, the operations of large-scale ranchers – the "Cattle Barons" – had dominated life on the plains. Small ranchers and farmers, or "homesteaders", often lived in fear of their land being squeezed out or swallowed up by the baron's vast holdings. This was true throughout the ranching states and territories – Colorado, Montana, Dakota, Nebraska, Kansas and Wyoming – where in 1892 the ongoing struggle erupted into a violent confrontation known as the Johnson County War

The cattle barons had a nasty habit of having anyone who stood up to them declared, publicly and loudly, a rustler. These rustlers, they reasoned, had to be stopped – which usually meant bringing in hired guns or vigilantes to do the job. In an 1889 precursor to the Johnson County violence, a rancher named A. J. Bothwell had designs on adjacent land along the Sweetwater River belonging to storekeeper James Averill and prostitute Ella Watson, Averill's companion and one-time lover.

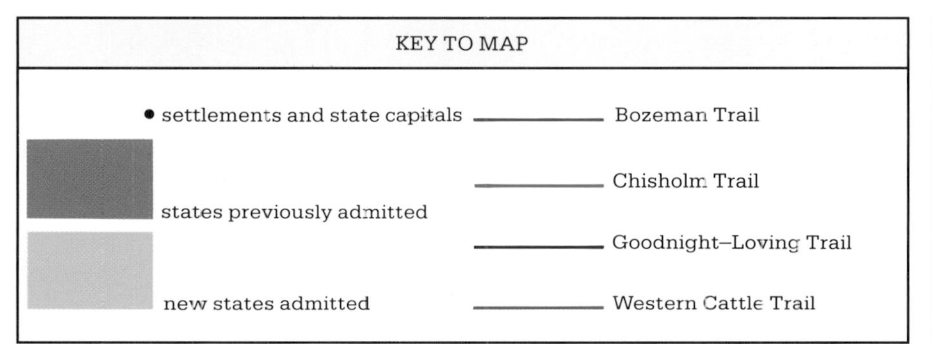

KEY TO MAP

| | |
|---|---|
| • settlements and state capitals | Bozeman Trail |
| | Chisholm Trail |
| states previously admitted | Goodnight–Loving Trail |
| new states admitted | Western Cattle Trail |

**OPPOSITE** A few years before long-simmering conflicts between large and small ranchers in the Western cattle country erupted in Wyoming's 1892 Johnson County Wars, prostitute Ella Watson – who often accepted cattle as payment – became embroiled in the struggle. In 1889, she and her companion Jim Averill (inset) were hauled in and lynched for cattle rustling; after Ella's death, a ranchers' smear campaign dubbed her "Cattle Kate".

**BELOW** A living symbol of the Great American West, the Texas Longhorn and other breeds of cattle literally covered the Great Plains between the 1870s and nineties when cattlemen and cowboys reigned supreme.

A few months after denouncing Bothwell as a land-grabber in the local paper and successfully disputing his claims, Averill – with Ella beside him – was declared a rustler by Bothwell and his cronies; both were lynched in front of their cabins in July, 1889. The cattlemen's propagandists turned Ella, a whore who had sometimes taken cattle in payment, into "Cattle Kate", an infamous rustler; the killers were never even brought to trial.

Three years later, a number of Johnson County cattle barons belonging to the Cheyenne Club engaged a small army of Texas hired guns to "invade" northern Wyoming and clear it of "rustlers". Led by cattlemen Major Frank Wolcott and W. C. Irvine on April 10, 1892, the cattlemen's army first went gunning through the snow for Johnson County Sheriff "Red" Angus who sided with the small ranchers, and then planned to eliminate everyone they called a rustler in three counties. Fortunately, Angus had caught wind of the plan and organized a force of his own. Only two victims – Nick Ray and Nate Champion – were killed by the invaders before Angus counter-attacked with a force of 300 farmers and small ranchers. Angus drove the cattlemen and their gunslingers back to their base at the TA ranch and kept them hemmed in there, until the invaders had to be rescued by the US Cavalry – called in at the request of the Cheyenne Club's political friends.

Public outcry after the Johnson County invasion reduced the power of the cattle barons, who never again dared to take the law into their own hands so boldly.

# The James–Younger Gang

The violence of the Civil War never ended for veterans like Jesse James (1847–82), his older brother Frank (1844–1915?) and the Younger Brothers, Cole, Bob and Jim – all of whom had ridden with bushwhacking Confederate guerilla units like the one led by William Quantrill in Missouri. Within a year of Robert E. Lee's April 1865 surrender to U.S. Grant at Appomattox, the James boys had begun – with a $60,000 haul from a bank in Liberty, Missouri – a string of armed robberies in southern and border states that would stretch over the next five years.

When Frank and Jesse were joined by the Youngers in about 1872, the combined brothers got into high gear, robbing banks, trains, stagecoaches, even steamboats. With a natural dislike of bankers, many citizens throughout the South enjoyed the exploits of the James–Younger gang, and the outlaws acquired a heroic quality as they took more loot – an eventual total of nearly half a million dollars – and more lives; at least 21 men died at the hands of the James–Younger gang.

Occasionally the gang's targets were in the North, as in the case of an Iowa robbery in 1871. It was on a raid deep into the North – at Northfield, Minnesota, on September 7, 1876 – that the James–Younger Gang finally had its comeuppance. Running into resistance from a handful of courageous townsmen, the gang had to shoot its way out of the town, and not everyone made it. Frank and Jesse did get away, but all three Youngers were captured and sent to prison, supposedly for life. Bob died in prison in 1889, but Cole and Jim were finally released in 1901, after 25 years in jail.

As for Jesse and Frank, each laid low for a while, but Jesse went back to robbery in 1879, prompting Missouri governor Thomas Crittenden to hire Robert Ford, a former James Gang member, secretly and get him to kill Jesse – which he did on April 3, 1882, reportedly shooting him in the back at his home. Frank lived on to a ripe old age – and even joined Cole Younger in a lecture tour about the evils of crime. But while they rode, the exploits of the James-Younger gang became the stuff of legend.

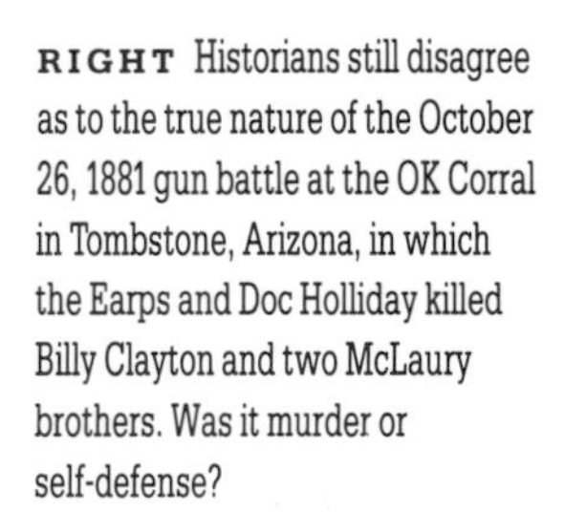

**RIGHT** Historians still disagree as to the true nature of the October 26, 1881 gun battle at the OK Corral in Tombstone, Arizona, in which the Earps and Doc Holliday killed Billy Clayton and two McLaury brothers. Was it murder or self-defense?

# The OK Corral

Perhaps one of the most famous – and misrepresented – occurrences in the often violent history of the West took place in Tombstone, Arizona, on October 26, 1881, at the OK Corral. Over a century of historical fiction has portrayed that incident as a classic showdown between lawmen and outlaws – a portrayal which can be termed inaccurate, if not downright false.

First of all, Tombstone's marshal Wyatt Earp, although a lawman with previous experience in Wichita and Dodge City, was not a paragon of virtue; he doubled as a faro dealer in a local saloon, and was only an adequate peace officer. His brothers Virgil, Morgan and James served as Wyatt's deputy, a stagecoach escort and a barkeeper, respectively. The Earps – and their alcoholic friend Doc Holliday, a dentist with a taste for murder, had been feuding with a hell-raising group of local cattlemen, including Billy and Ike Clanton and Frank and Tom McLaury, who did a bit of rustling on the side.

Far from fitting the popular description of a stand-off between good guys and bad guys, some historians consider the "Gunfight at the OK Corral" to be nothing but cold-blooded murder of the Clantons and McLaurys, some of whom were unarmed, by the Earps and Doc Holliday. The Earps always maintained that the show-down was fought in self-defense. In any case, Billy Clanton and both McLaurys were killed, while Ike Clanton just missed being blown away by a shotgun blast from Holliday, who was also wounded along with Morgan and Virgil Earp.

Less than a year after the OK Corral incident, Morgan Earp was killed in an ambush. In response Wyatt and Holliday tracked down and shot the two men they considered to be Morgan's killers, and were forced to elude a pursuing posse in Colorado. Wyatt Earp lived on until 1929 – but will always be remembered as the "hero" of the OK Corral".

# The Oklahoma Guardsmen

The Oklahoma Land Rushes in the late 1880s had been one signal that the American West was closing fast. By the mid-1890s what had once been the Indian Territory was now close to being settled by whites, and within a decade it would become the state of Oklahoma. At about this time, a trio of superb lawmen were "cleaning up" in Oklahoma, trying to bring law and order to one of the last frontiers left in the American West. In time, they came to be known as the "Three Guardsmen": Bill Tilghman, Chris Madsen and Heck Thomas.

Tilghman, whose reputation as a crack shot and buffalo hunter preceded him, served first as a Dodge City Marshal before coming to Oklahoma as a deputy US Marshal. He was crafty and cool, but also had a fine sense of humor – it was Tilghman who administered

**NEAR LEFT** "Uncle Billy" Tilghman was an intelligent, resourceful and persistent lawman who chased the Doolin Gang, the Dalton Gang and the Starr Gang, contributing to the demise of all three.

**MIDDLE LEFT** Tough Scandinavian Chris Madsen fought for three countries before becoming one of the "three guardsmen" – with the Italian insurgent Garibaldi, the French Foreign Legion and with the US cavalry against Indian resistance.

**FAR LEFT** Heck Thomas began his eventful career as a 12-year-old courier for the Confederacy, turning his hand to private detective work before being signed on as deputy to Oklahoma's US Marshal Evett Nix in 1893.

a spanking to Jennie "Little Britches" Stevens instead of shooting her.

Danish-born Chris Madsen came to the trio after distinguished military service for three nations – with Italian insurgent Garibaldi, with the French Foreign Legion and, after arriving in America in 1870, with the US Cavalry against the Indian Resistance.

The final member of this trio, Georgian Heck Thomas, started his adventures as a 12-year-old courier for the Confederacy. Thomas, who was "murder" with a shotgun, had also worked as a private detective before hiring on as a deputy to Oklahoma's US Marshal Evett Nix in 1893.

The Guardsmen were to become a figure of nemesis for just one man in Oklahoma in the '90s – a one-time Arkansas farmhand named Bill Doolin, a member of the infamous Dalton gang who had luckily missed the Coffeyville, Kansas raid that ended the lives of most of the Dalton gang on October 5, 1892. It was Tilghman who first captured Doolin by catching him unawares in an Arkansas mineral bathhouse in 1895, dressed as a preacher. When Doolin went for his gun, Tilghman talked him out of resisting. But Doolin soon escaped and it was Heck Thomas who caught up with him with a posse in 1896. Cornered, Bill Doolin swung around, aimed at Thomas – and missed; Thomas's shotgun put Doolin away for good.

# A GALLERY OF LAWMEN

### IRA ATEN (?–1953)

Joining the fabled Texas Rangers in 1884, Aten rounded up badmen of all kinds in five years. He moved on to serve as a lawman in various parts of Texas, keeping rustlers off ranch lands and generally keeping the peace. Based in California from the turn of the century, he died in 1953.

### WILD BILL HICKOK (1837–76)

Yes, the famed spy, scout and Indian fighter was also a lawman; but as the US Marshal in Abilene, Kansas, in 1871, Hickok's trigger-happy reputation (earned after accidentally killing a deputy) – coupled with Abilene's decline as an important cattle town – lost him the job.

### BAT MASTERSON (?–1921)

This dapper gambler had a side career as a lawman; a crack shot, he served as a marshal in Dodge City and in Colorado, then gambled in Denver and cheated in New York, where he wound up a sports-writer and died in 1921.

**RIGHT** Celebrated lawman Wyatt Earp (seated, second from left) was photographed in the late 1870s with other members of the Dodge City, Kansas, Peace Commission, including Bat Masterson (standing at right).

Rough justice . . . In this famous photo, Judge Roy Bean (seated on a beer keg and wearing a sombrero) tries a horse thief at his unpretentious court at his saloon in Langtry, Texas, in 1900.

**LEFT** After election to the US House of Representatives as a Republican, Isaac C. Parker was appointed judge of the western district of Arizona, an unruly area that included the Indian Territory in its jurisdiction. Parker's rigorous justice helped to bring law and order to the area.

### ISAAC C. PARKER: THE HANGING JUDGE (?-1896)

After taking over the Indian Territory district known as "Robber's Roost", Parker transformed the region by employing such lawmen as the Three Guardsmen and sentencing many desperadoes to hang on the multiple gallows he had built. The tireless judge had effectively "cleaned up" the territory by the time it became part of Oklahoma; he died, probably of exhaustion, at the age of 57 in 1896.

### JOHN SLAUGHTER

A former Texas Ranger, Slaughter gained his reputation as a shotgun-wielding sheriff in Cochise County, Arizona, cleaning up that hotbed of rustling and robbery.

**LEFT** In the Old West, justice was often summary and brutal. In Tombstone, Arizona, in 1884, John Heith was implicated in a store robbery in which four people were killed – and lynched. His five confederates were caught and legally hanged at Tombstone one month later.

# WARRIORS, CHIEFS AND SOLDIERS

The Indian Wars, as they were called, effectively raged on for most of the 19th century – although European Americans had been contesting the land of Native Americans since the 16th century. The 19th century saw the resistance of Native Americans crushed by the military might of the US, beginning at Horseshoe Bend in 1814 and ending in the tragedy at Wounded Knee more than 75 years later.

## Horseshoe Bend

The War of 1812 between the US and Britain was not yet over when an important battle forecast what lay in store for the Native American nations in the new century. Even before the Battle of New Orleans, which made him a national hero in 1815, General Andrew Jackson was leading American troops to victory in the South over another enemy – the Creek nation. The Creeks were a great Native American confederacy spread throughout the South; many tribes had remained neutral during the war with the British, but some had fought the Americans actively. One such tribe was led by Red Eagle (born William Weatherford, of Indian and Scotch ancestry).

In August 1813 Red Eagle launched a raid on Fort Mims on the Alabama River in which most of the white inhabitants were killed. Responding to the attack, the US sent a force of 3,500 under General Jackson to the Alabama; Davy Crockett was among them.

The forces clashed in the woods in November, but the battle was indecisive. After the winter had passed, Jackson's troops marched again, this time to a part of the Tallapoosa River known as Horseshoe Bend – there they effectively destroyed the Creek nation. Following the battle, the defeated Red Eagle crossed the American lines alone and surrendered himself to Jackson. Impressed, Jackson allowed Red Eagle to go free – but he would never fight again. His Creeks, who lost some 20 million acres of land as a result of the battle, were just the first of virtually every tribe to lose their ancestral home.

**OPPOSITE LEFT** What he started, by breaking the strength of the Creek Nation at Horseshoe Bend in 1814, Andrew Jackson finished in the 1830s as the seventh President of the United States – the Removal of the "Five Civilized Tribes".

**ABOVE** The courageous surrender of Creek chief William Weatherford, alias Red Eagle – who walked alone and unarmed into General Andrew Jackson's camp after the 1814 Battle of Horseshoe Bend – signified the loss of 20 million acres of Creek land, and much of the power and pride of the Creek Confederacy.

## The Trail of Tears

Not long after the War of 1812 ended, white settlers began moving westward from the eastern seaboard into land that had belonged to Native Americans for centuries. By 1830, the US Government – headed by Andrew Jackson of the Horseshoe Bend victory, now the President – began legislating the south-eastern Indians out of their homelands. It was called the Removal – a forced march by which the "Five Civilized Tribes" (Creek, Cherokee, Seminole, Chickasaw and Choctaw) would leave their land for the "Indian Territory" (later to become Oklahoma).

Some of the nations began to leave their territory in the early 1830s, but the mighty Cherokee nation resisted. Under the leadership of their Chief, John Ross, the Cherokees fought the Removal policy right up to the Supreme Court – but in the end they too were forced to migrate from their homes in Georgia and Tennessee, beginning in the late 1830s.

The Cherokee Removal proved the most difficult and heartbreaking of all. The elements, illness, mistreatment and neglect plagued the Cherokee people as they trudged across hundreds of miles to the Indian Territory. Nearly one quarter of the Cherokee emigrants died on the way – and the journey will be known for ever as the Trail of Tears.

# War in the West

As the American population progressed westward in the 1840s and '50s, the US Army tried to keep those Native American nations that were not already subdued in check, and well away from the hundreds of emigrants then moving across the continent. But in the 1860s – when the army was preoccupied with the Civil War in the East – a number of Indian nations took an opportunity to mount their resistance anew, including the Minnesota Sioux to the north and the Navajos and Apaches in the south-west.

In 1861, an incident involving a kidnapped American boy and a case of mistaken identity among Apache bands sparked a confrontation between the US Army and a chief of the Chiricahua Apaches, Cochise, whose family was left in the hands of soldiers who would not exchange prisoners. As a result, Cochise executed his prisoners and, in turn, his brother was hanged. Going on the warpath, Cochise's warriors staged raid after raid on American settlements in Arizona, killing hundreds.

**RIGHT** Grim-faced in this Army portrait, General Oliver O. Howard played a pivotal role in making both war and peace in several Western theaters of operations. In the South-west in 1872, Howard negotiated a treaty with Chiricahua Apache chief Cochise. Five years later, it was he who forced the noble Nez Perce leader Chief Joseph into war.

**OPPOSITE TOP** Although an eccentric in dress and personal habits and a lover of publicity, General George Crook was among the most able and dedicated commanders in the Army of the West. Decent and humane, he was described by General W. T. Sherman as "the greatest Indian fighter and manager the Army ever had".

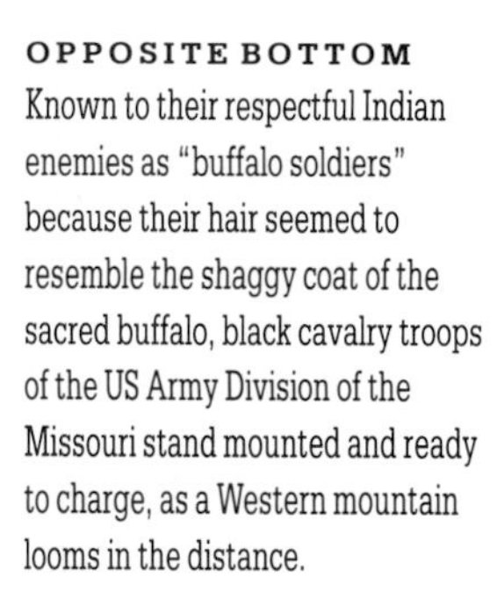

**OPPOSITE BOTTOM** Known to their respectful Indian enemies as "buffalo soldiers" because their hair seemed to resemble the shaggy coat of the sacred buffalo, black cavalry troops of the US Army Division of the Missouri stand mounted and ready to charge, as a Western mountain looms in the distance.

Settlers, ranchers, traders and drivers all scattered out of the territory in the face of the onslaught – with the exception of a mail superintendent named Tom Jeffords. Because his mail drivers were being picked off one by one, the courageous, red-haired Jeffords rode – alone – to see Cochise at his encampment. Startled and impressed, Cochise admired Jeffords' courage, the two became friends, and Jeffords' drivers werer left alone. But the struggle between the Americans and the Apaches went on for years.

Following a massacre of Apaches by whites in 1871, public pressure prompted the Government to send General George Crook and General Oliver O. Howard to the South-west to make peace with Cochise and the Apaches. With Tom Jeffords' help, peace was made with Cochise and the Apaches at their mountain stronghold in 1872; it held for several years – until the time of another Apache warrior chief, Geronimo.

## THE GREAT SOLDIERS

These great military leaders were instrumental in "winning" the West in the 18th and 19th centuries.

### GEORGE CROOK (1828-90)

Led series of campaigns against the Apache, correcting the Army's lack of mobility by using mules for supply. Crook recruited friendly Apaches to help hunt down hostiles and also conducted operations against the Sioux; he served some 20 years in the West.

### WILLIAM HENRY HARRISON: "OLD TIPPECANOE" (1773-1841)

Harrison earned his title as victor over Tecumseh at Tippecanoe in 1811; he was also Governor of Indian Territory and 9th President of the US.

### ANDREW JACKSON (1767-1845)

As a US Army general Jackson broke Creek power at Horseshoe Bend, won victories over the British in the War of 1812; and, as 7th President, forced the Removal of south-eastern tribes and enacted Draconian anti-Indian policies.

**BELOW AND INSET**
Although General Philip Sheridan has been credited with the phrase, "the only good Indian is a dead Indian," the Army's top Western commander during the Indian Wars once expressed another opinion: "We took away their country, broke up their mode of living . . . introduced disease and decay among them, and it was for this and against this that they made war. Could anyone expect less?"

### ROBERT ROGERS (1731–95)

The 18th-century prototype of the "Indian fighter", he led "Rogers' Rangers" during the French and Indian War. He fought for the British in the Revolution; and is said to have been the model for Hawkeye in James Fenimore Cooper's famous novel, *The Last of the Mohicans.*

### PHILIP SHERIDAN (1831–88)

Another Civil War commander; Sheridan succeeded Sherman as Commander of the US forces in the West. He made the infamous remark, "The only good Indian is a dead Indian."

**BELOW LEFT** Famed for the burning of Atlanta and his "march to the sea" during the Civil War, General W. T. Sherman became Commanding General of the entire US Army between 1866 and 1869.

### WILLIAM TECUMSEH SHERMAN (1820–91)

A Civil War commander who took command of the US military forces in the West after the war. He undertook the building of forts across the West to aid in westward expansion; and set the military policy for pushing Indians out of their lands.

### ZACHARY TAYLOR: "OLD ROUGH AND READY" (1784–1850)

Brigadier-General in the Mexican War, which forced Mexico to give California and the New Mexico Territory to the US, Taylor later lived less than one year as the 12th President of the US.

**BELOW** General Zachary Taylor spent four decades in the US Army before succeeding Polk as the 12th President of the US.

## The Minnesota Sioux Uprising

During the summer of 1862, the Santee Sioux, confined to a reservation along the Minnesota River, were simmering. Frustrated at their confinement, the lack of game, unscrupulous white traders and other injustices, matters came to a head for some Santee on August 17. Four young braves dared each other to kill a few white men, and thereupon shot and killed five settlers. The next day, led by their chief, Little Crow, the Santee went on a rampage, burning homes, raping, pillaging and murdering nearly 400 settlers, and sending some 200 refugees scrambling for the protection of Fort Ridgely across the river. A few days later, Little Crow repeatedly attacked the fort but was repulsed; his warriors then launched an assault on New Ulm, reducing the village to ashes and forcing the survivors to evacuate.

The uprising was finally quelled a month later when troops under Colonel H. H. Sibley defeated Little Crow's warriors on September 23. The chief himself escaped, only to be shot and killed by a farmer some time later. Sibley's troopers rounded up about 2,000 Santee, tried nearly 400 for atrocities and sentenced 303 of them to hang. Before the sentences could be carried out, however, President Lincoln commuted the sentences of all the Santees except 38; these, convicted of murder and rape, were hanged in the largest mass execution in American history.

Terrifying as it was, the Santee uprising was not such a terribly uncommon event; Native Americans throughout the West had grievances similar to those of the Santee, and their frustrations also erupted into violence.

## Little Bighorn

The 1870s and '80s witnessed scores of battles between US troops and Native American forces from many nations across the West. The most legendary, perhaps, is that which took place on June 25, 1876 near the Little Bighorn River in Montana Territory. The American unit involved was the 7th Cavalry, commanded by Lieutenant-Colonel George Armstrong Custer, a flamboyant Civil War hero who had been reduced from Major-General to Lieutenant-Colonel in the post-war Army, and temporarily lost his command after implicating President Grant's brother in a scandal. When Custer led his contingent into the area on June 22 his intention was to engage and hopefully entrap a large force of Indians. On one count, he was to get his way: his 600-odd troops would soon face a combined force of Sioux and Northern Cheyenne warriors that numbered between 2,500 and 3,000 men – possibly the largest single force of Native American warriors ever assembled.

After marching his men some 40 miles, Custer approached a Sioux-Cheyenne village on the Little Bighorn. Instead of heeding his scouts' warnings of a vastly superior Indian force and waiting for reinforcements, Custer divided his forces. Taking one contingent himself, Custer dispatched Captain Frederic Benteen and Major Marcus Reno to take up positions across Ash Creek. Ordering the attack, Custer had Reno's troops charge the village, and all hell broke loose. Surprised by a large force commanded by the Hunkpapa chief Gall at his flank and rear, Custer was pummeled on the other side by Oglala Sioux chief Crazy Horse; completing the attack, Low Dog, another Oglala Sioux, fended off Reno's men and closed in on General Custer.

Known for ever after as "Custer's Last Stand", the Battle of Little Bighorn was among the greatest disasters in the history of the American military; not one of Custer's men was left alive. For the Indian forces who captured the day, it was perhaps the greatest victory ever won by a Native American force.

**LEFT** George Armstrong Custer – a general in the Civil War, but a colonel when he and his entire regiment met their deaths in the legendary 1876 Battle of Little Bighorn – seen here in uncharacteristic buckskins. He was pehaps the most famous of all "Indian Fighters", and was publicly mourned as a hero. But the men who served with and under him knew otherwise; although he may have been brave, Custer was a poor commander; a vain, impulsive gloryseeker who put his own comfort and ego first, with little regard for his men's welfare – as his final, fatal campaign attests.

# The End Comes: The Ghost Dance and Wounded Knee

**ABOVE** General Nelson Miles shared the opinion of Generals Sherman and Sheridan that Indians were savages. Tough and uncompromising, Miles served long and well in the Army's Indian campaigns: in 1877, in the crackdown on the Sioux following Little Bighorn; later that year, forcing the surrender of Nez Perce Chief Joseph; and more than a decade later when Miles arrested the Sioux chief Sitting Bull, in the incident that would lead to the tragic massacre at Wounded Knee in 1890.

**RIGHT** Chief Sitting Bull, of the Teton Sioux, photographed around 1885. Absolutely fearless, Sitting Bull was a warrior by the time he was 14 years old.

By the end of the 1880s, the "Red Man" had been driven off most of his lands and on to reservations. The Native American peoples lived for the most part in poverty, vulnerable to epidemics, drought, starvation and despair. But in 1889 a Paiute shaman (or holy man) named Wovoka told tribal leaders that he had seen a vision of a world in which peace, the buffalo and the Indians' fallen comrades would return; he declared that the white man would disappear, and the red man would carry on in a blissful life. The key to this new religion was a ritual dance – which whites called the "Ghost Dance" – and it gave new hope to thousands of desperate Native Americans.

The Ghost Dance cult spread across the reservations of the West. When it reached the Sioux in the Dakotas, the worshippers – fearing that the Government would ban their new religion – adopted the wearing of "ghost shirts" painted with magic symbols to ward off evil spirits and attackers' bullets. Although one perceptive American – former Army doctor and Indian agent Valentine McGillycuddy – believed that the dance was harmless and should be allowed to continue, most Indian agents and Government authorities felt threatened by the cult.

Acting upon agents' fears about the Ghost Dance frenzy that was sweeping the reservations, the Army sent troops to the Pine Ridge agency in the fall of 1890. In December, Major-General Nelson Miles arrested the Hunkpapa Sioux chief Sitting Bull at the Cheyenne River Reservation, on the erroneous grounds that the famed warrior and medicine-man had started the Ghost Dance cult as a way to stir unrest. When Indian police arrested the great chief, a scuffle ensued, and Sitting Bull and several other Sioux were killed. Reacting to the killing, hundreds of Hunkpapa fled, and eventually tried to evade Army surveillance by sneaking off to the Pine Ridge agency – but were pursued by Federal troops.

**ABOVE** In mute testimony to the slaughter of several hundred Sioux men, women and children near Wounded Knee Creek in the Pine Ridge Reservation on December 29, 1890, the frozen body of Miniconiou Sioux chief Big Foot lies silently in the Dakota snow.

**RIGHT** In part because he paid no heed to a scout's report that an overwhelming Sioux force was nearby, George Armstrong Custer – whose men called him "Hard Ass" – led hundreds of men to their deaths at the Little Bighorn. Today, the tombstones of the fallen dot the Montana site, preserved as a National Monument.

On December 28, 1890, the Indians camped at Wounded Knee Creek, some 20 miles from the Pine Ridge agency – and about 500 soldiers surrounded them to prevent an escape. The officer in command ordered the Indians to surrender their weapons; when they refused he had the tepees – and the Indians themselves – searched. A scuffle broke out and one of the Indians fired a wild shot – setting off a volley from the troops surrounding the Indians. More Indians returned fire, and the troops opened up with Hotchkiss machine-guns and shot anything that moved – including women and children. When the smoke cleared, about 25 soldiers had been killed, mostly by their own crossfire. But the Indians had been slaughtered – anything between 150 and 300 men, women and children were killed at Wounded Knee. Incredibly, the Army awarded the Congressional Medal of Honor to dozens of soldiers for "valor" in the "Battle" of Wounded Knee. But Wounded Knee was not a battle; it was a massacre which tragically marked the end of Native American resistance in the western United States.

KEY TO MAP

- ■ fort
- ▲ Indian agency
- ★ Indian battle
- Bozeman Trail
- Chisholm Trail
- Goodnight–Loving Trail
- Western Cattle Trail

## GREAT WARRIORS, GREAT CHIEFS

Scores of Native American tribes were led by many extraordinary men throughout the 18th and 19th centuries; here are just a few of these great chiefs.

### RED CLOUD (OGLALA SIOUX; 1822–1909)

This courageous Sioux warrior opposed westward expansion by whites; he strove to defend hunting-grounds, closing down the Bozeman Trail and other overland routes west. Red Cloud signed the Fort Laramie Treaty in 1868 and forced the US to keep its terms.

**BELOW RIGHT** Geronimo, the famous Chiricuhua Apache chief who waged an effective guerrilla war in the South-west against both Americans and Mexicans.

### GERONIMO (APACHE; 1829–1909)

Born Goyathlay, he was perhaps the most famous 19th-century Indian; Geronimo led Apache resistance from 1876 to 1884, when peace was made with Crook; he led a further uprising from 1885–7; and lived on reservation after 1887.

### CRAZY HORSE (SIOUX; *c.* 1841–77)

Born Tashunka Witco, Crazy Horse was perhaps the greatest of the Sioux chiefs. He hated whites and took part in nearly all the major battles fought by the Sioux (Rosebud, Little Bighorn, etc.); he surrendered to Crook in 1877.

### BLACK HAWK (SAUK; 1767–1838)

A great Sauk warrior and leader who opposed the cession of Sauk/Fox lands east of the Mississippi to the US. He fought with the British in the War of 1812; and in 1832 fought, and was defeated, in the Black Hawk War against US. Black Hawk met President Andrew Jackson in 1833.

### CAPTAIN JACK (MODOC; *c.* 1837–73)

Born Kintpuash, Captain Jack led Modoc resistance to Removal in the "Modoc War", 1872–3; at the behest of other Modoc who later betrayed him, Kintpuash killed General Canby; he and other Modocs were later executed in 1873.

**LEFT** The courageous Sioux chief Red Cloud led a delegation to Washington to try to negotiate an end to trespassing by goldseekers on the Sioux reservation in the Black Hills.

**ABOVE** A resistance leader of the Modoc tribe of the Pacific Northwest, Kintpuash – nicknamed "Captain Jack" for the military uniform coat he often wore – was instrumental in the Modoc War of 1872–73.

**CHIEF JOSEPH (NEZ PERCE; *c.* 1832–1904)**
This Great Nez Perce chief, born Hinmaton Yalatkit became a skilled military leader of non-treaty Nez Perce. He won 18 battles in the 1877 war, then led the retreat to Canada brilliantly, before surrending to Miles in 1877. Chief Joseph met with McKinley, Miles and Howard in 1897, and President Roosevelt in 1903.

**OSCEOLA (SEMINOLE; *c.* 1804–38)**
Organizer of the Seminole resistance against Removal which began the Second Seminole War (1835–42). Osceola led a guerilla war against American troops brilliantly; he agreed to a conference under a flag of truce, but was captured and died in prison in 1838.

**OURAY (UTE; *c.* 1820–80)**
A Spanish-speaking Ute chief who worked closely with the American Government, especially Kit Carson, in the 1860s and '70s; he intervened in the Nathan Meeker killing controversy.

**PONTIAC (OTTAWA; *c.* 1720–69)**
A leading force behind a series of coordinated attacks on British outposts in the Great Lakes in the 1760s, he was a major proponent of Indian unity against the whites west of the Appalachians. Pontiac was murdered by a Peoria warrior at Cahokia, Illinois.

**ABOVE** With the final words, "I will fight no more forever," Chief Joseph of the Nez Perce surrendered his warriors to General Nelson Miles just short of the Canadian border in 1877, after a legendary trek from his people's homeland in Washington state.

**RIGHT** Although a tireless defender of his people's rights, the Uncompaghre Ute chief Ouray – "The Arrow" – was among the most supportive Native American leaders the US Government ever encountered.

**SEQUOYAH (CHEROKEE; 1776–1843)**
A brilliant scholar and developer of Cherokee "syllabary" or alphabet, Sequoyah published the first Native American-language newspaper, the Cherokee *Phoenix*. He overcame early alcoholism to become a fine craftsman and journalist. Sequoia trees are named after him.

**TECUMSEH (SHAWNEE; *c.* 1768–1813)**
One of the greatest Native American leaders ever and a strong opponent of the United States; Tecumseh strove for a united Native American nation, the Indian Confederacy, to rival the US; he fought with the British during the war of 1812 and was killed in action at the age of 44.

**LEFT** The Cherokee intellectual Sequoyah, seen here with the written syllabary he devised around 1821. California giant redwoods are named after him.

**BELOW** A fanciful portrayal of a stand-off between the great Shawnee chief Tecumseh and Northwest Territory governor (later US President) William Henry Harrison at their futile 1810 conference.

# WILD WEST TIME CHART

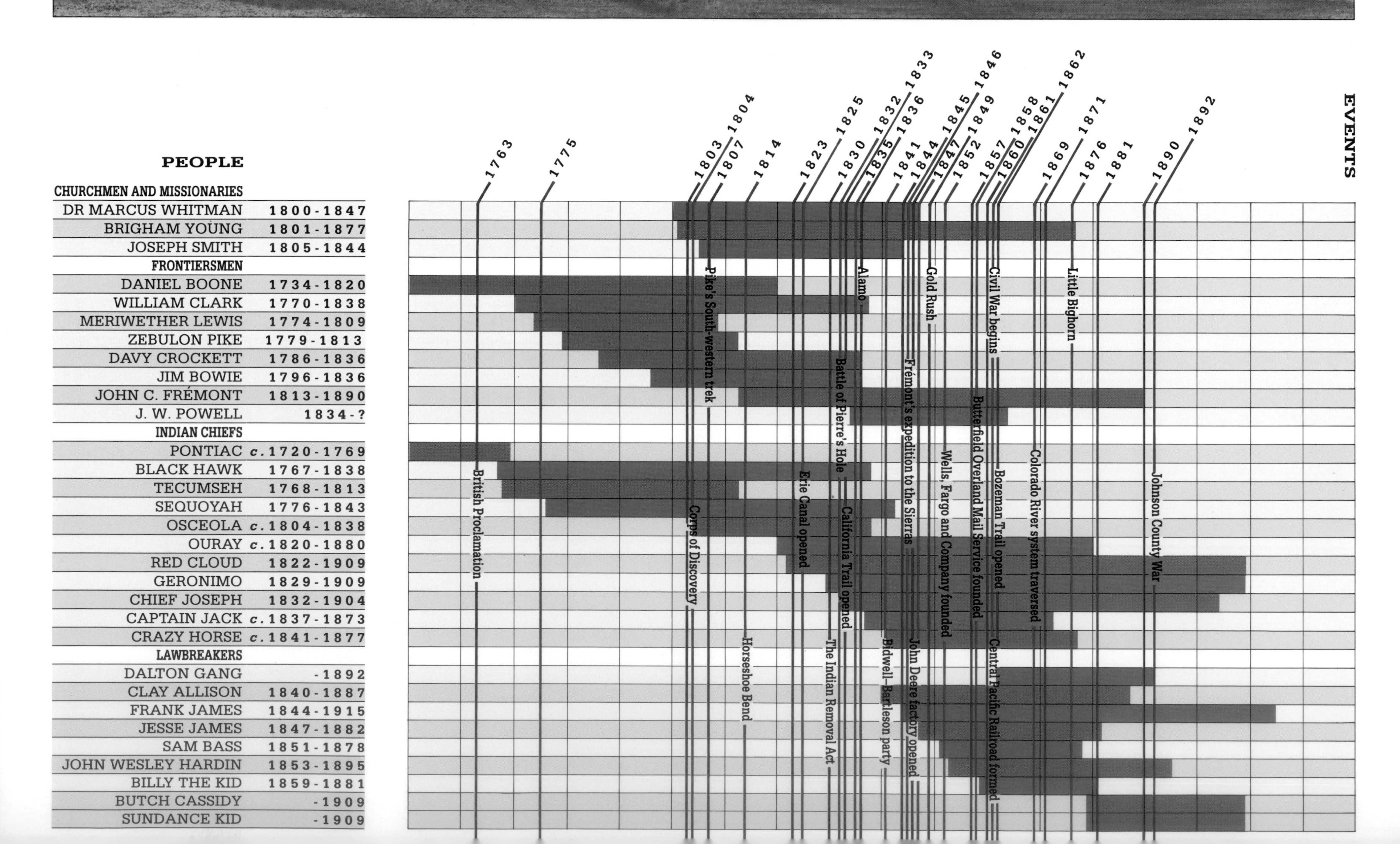

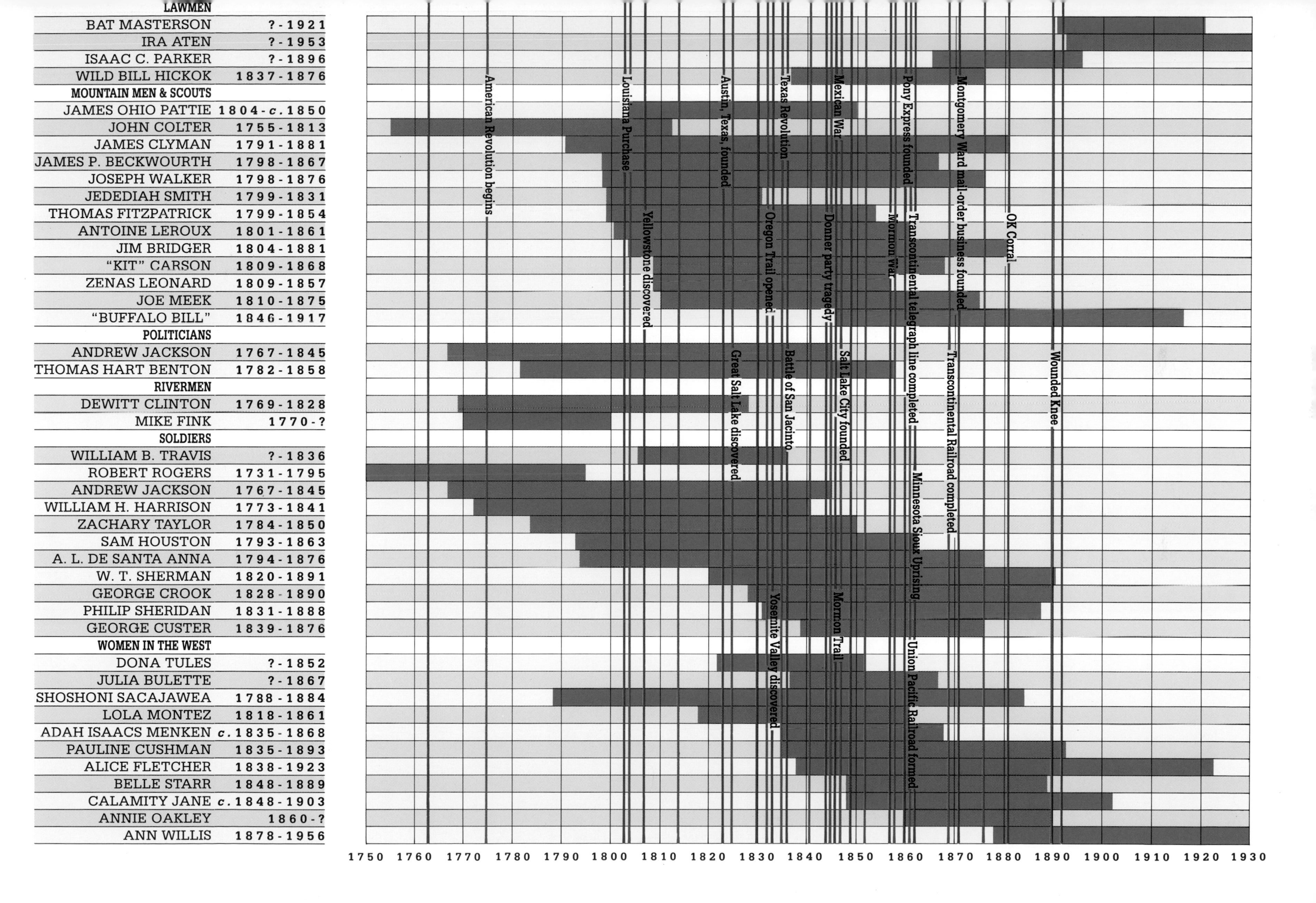
LAWMEN
BAT MASTERSON ?-1921
IRA ATEN ?-1953
ISAAC C. PARKER ?-1896
WILD BILL HICKOK 1837-1876
MOUNTAIN MEN & SCOUTS
JAMES OHIO PATTIE 1804-c.1850
JOHN COLTER 1755-1813
JAMES CLYMAN 1791-1881
JAMES P. BECKWOURTH 1798-1867
JOSEPH WALKER 1798-1876
JEDEDIAH SMITH 1799-1831
THOMAS FITZPATRICK 1799-1854
ANTOINE LEROUX 1801-1861
JIM BRIDGER 1804-1881
"KIT" CARSON 1809-1868
ZENAS LEONARD 1809-1857
JOE MEEK 1810-1875
"BUFFALO BILL" 1846-1917
POLITICIANS
ANDREW JACKSON 1767-1845
THOMAS HART BENTON 1782-1858
RIVERMEN
DEWITT CLINTON 1769-1828
MIKE FINK 1770-?
SOLDIERS
WILLIAM B. TRAVIS ?-1836
ROBERT ROGERS 1731-1795
ANDREW JACKSON 1767-1845
WILLIAM H. HARRISON 1773-1841
ZACHARY TAYLOR 1784-1850
SAM HOUSTON 1793-1863
A. L. DE SANTA ANNA 1794-1876
W. T. SHERMAN 1820-1891
GEORGE CROOK 1828-1890
PHILIP SHERIDAN 1831-1888
GEORGE CUSTER 1839-1876
WOMEN IN THE WEST
DONA TULES ?-1852
JULIA BULETTE ?-1867
SHOSHONI SACAJAWEA 1788-1884
LOLA MONTEZ 1818-1861
ADAH ISAACS MENKEN c.1835-1868
PAULINE CUSHMAN 1835-1893
ALICE FLETCHER 1838-1923
BELLE STARR 1848-1889
CALAMITY JANE c.1848-1903
ANNIE OAKLEY 1860-?
ANN WILLIS 1878-1956
American Revolution begins
Louisiana Purchase
Yellowstone discovered
Austin, Texas, founded
Great Salt Lake discovered
Oregon Trail opened
Yosemite Valley discovered
Texas Revolution
Battle of San Jacinto
Donner party tragedy
Mexican War
Salt Lake City founded
Mormon Trail
Mormon War
Pony Express founded
Transcontinental telegraph line completed
Minnesota Sioux Uprising
Union Pacific Railroad formed
Transcontinental Railroad completed
Montgomery Ward mail-order business founded
OK Corral
Wounded Knee
1750 1760 1770 1780 1790 1800 1810 1820 1830 1840 1850 1860 1870 1880 1890 1900 1910 1920 1930

# INDEX

*Italic* page numbers refer to picture captions

# BIBLIOGRAPHY

Adams, James Truslow, ed., *Atlas of American History* (New York: Charles Scribner's Sons, 1943).
Barnard, Edward S., ed., *Reader's Digest Story of the Great American West* (Pleasantville, NY: Reader's Digest, 1977).
Brown, Dee, *The Westerners* (New York: Holt, Rinehart and Winston, 1974).
Dockstader, Frederick J., *Great North American Indians: Profiles in Life and Leadership* (New York: Van Nostrand Reinhold, 1977).
Dunlop, Richard, *Great Trails of the West* (Nashville, Tenn.: Abingdon Press, 1971).
Froncek, Thomas, ed., *Voices from the Wilderness: The Frontiersman's Own Story* (New York: McGraw-Hill, 1974).
Gilbert, Bill and the Editors of Time-Life Books, *The Trailblazers* (The Old West series) (New York: Time-Life Books, 1973).
Hewitt, James, ed., *Eye-Witnesses to Wagon Trains West* (New York: Charles Scribner's Sons, 1973).
Horan, James D., *The Gunfighters: The Authentic Wild West* (New York: Crown Publishers, 1976).
Horan, James D. and Paul Sann, *Pictorial History of the Wild West* (New York: Crown Publishers, 1954).
Horn, Huston and the Editors of Time-Life Books, *The Pioneers* (The Old West series) (New York: Time-Life Books, 1974).
Josephy, Alvin M. Jr., *The Patriot Chiefs* (New York: The Viking Press, 1961).
Kagan, Hilde Heun and the Editors of American Heritage, *The American Heritage Pictorial Atlas of United States History* (New York: American Heritage, 1966).
Lavender, David and the Editors of American Heritage, *The American Heritage History of the Great West* (New York: American Heritage, 1965).
May, Robin, *The Story of the Wild West* (London: Hamlyn, 1978).
Morgan, Dale L. *Rand McNally's Pioneer Atlas of the American West* (Chicago: Rand McNally, 1956).
Nevin, David and the Editors of Time-Life Books, *The Soldiers* (The Old West series) (New York: Time-Life Books, 1978).
Ray, Grace Ernestine, *Wily Women of the West* (San Antonio, Texas: The Naylor Company, 1972).
Schmitt, Martin F. and Dee Brown, *Fighting Indians of the West* (New York: Bonanza Books, 1948).
Shenkman, Richard, *Legends, Lies and Cherished Myths of American History* (New York: William Morrow, 1988).
Tanner, Ogden and the Editors of Time-Life Books, *The Ranchers* (The Old West series) (Alexandria, Virginia: Time-Life Books, 1977).
Utley, Robert M. and Wilcomb E. Washburn, *The American Heritage History of the Indian Wars* (New York: American Heritage, 1977).
Wheeler, Keith and the Editors of Time-Life Books, *The Chroniclers* (The Old West series) (New York: Time-Life Books, 1976).
Wheeler, Keith and the Editors of Time-Life Books, *The Scouts* (The Old West series) (Alexandria, Virginia: Time-Life Books, 1978).

# PICTURE CREDITS

t = top; b = bottom; r = right; l = left.

**Stuart Atchinson:** pp.2–3. **Union Pacific Museum Collection:** 6–7 (no. 8–110), 68–9 (no. 5–135). **Library of Congress:** 8, 16, 17, 19t, 28, 32t, 40, 56t, 61, 64b, 65, 71, 73, 74, 75l, 79b, 81b, 82b, 92, 93, 94t, 95t, 97r, 99, 100, 105l, 107b. **Cumberland Gap National Historical Park:** 10, **Virginia Division of Tourism:** 11. **Fort Clatsop National Park:** 12, 13, 15. **Colorado Tourism Board:** 14. **National Archives:** 19b, 35t, 37t, 52, 54b, 56b, 57b, 62b, 64t, 68t, 69t, 90, 91b, 96, 97l, 101, 102t, 104r, 105r, 106. **Photo/Nats – Don Johnston:** 20. **Wyoming Travel Commission:** 21. **Photo/Nats – A. Peter Margosian:** 22–3. **Kansas State Historical Society:** 23t, 29. **Colorado Historical Society:** 24, 26, 53, 54t, 55b, 79t. **Fort Union National Monument:** 27. **Trevor Wood:** 30. **Joslyn Art Museum:** 31. **Canyon de Chelly National Monument:** 32b. **Latter-Day Saints:** 34–5, 36t, 37b. **Scott T. Smith:** 36b, 39. **Wyoming Division of Tourism:** 38. **John Deere Company:** 41. **Montgomery Ward:** 42. **Bent's Fort/Pat Trahey:** 43. **The Daughters of the Republic of Texas Library:** 44, 50, 51b. **Archives Division – Texas State Library:** 48, 51t, 81t, 82t. **Marshall Gold Discovery Site National Historical Park:** 56t, 57t. **Pony Express Historical Association:** 58. **North Wind Picture Archive:** 58–9, 62–3t. **Golden Spike National Historical Society:** 66–7. **American Heritage Center, University of Wyoming:** 70, 80b, 83, 84. **Henry Huntingdon Library:** 72. **Oklahoma Historical Society:** 75r, 88, 89, 91t, 104l. **Jeanne Kidd:** 78, 86–7. **Museum of New Mexico:** 80t. **Photo/Nats – Ann Reilly:** 85. **The National Park Service: Fort Davis National Historical Site:** 94b. **Custer Battlefield National Historical Park:** 102b. **Great Smokey Mountains National Park:** 107t.